creativity TODAY

tools for a creative attitude for business, education, industry, training, development, government, consultants, workers, thinkers, meetings, co-creation, design, health, sustainable growth, handling costs, art, technology, raising children, production, peace keeping, city marketing, peak performance, flower arrangement, dialogue, business blind dates, sports, pharmaceuticals, writers, travelling, reducing risk aversion, cleaners, experimentation, globalists, industry cross-overs, profitable losses, networks, commercial care, brotherhood, architects, strategy, religion, wealth, marketing, distribution, fashion, space discovery, company jesters, administration, corporate soul, nature, stubborn people, cultural diversity, media coaching, lovers, politics, let, water management, United Nations, carement, cooking, prosumers, rappers, faciggling,

**Now including
CREATION
TODAY**
new vision on
organisational
development
by Godelieve Spaas

Igor Byttebier & Ramon Vullings
BIS Publishers

creativity
TODAY

BIS Publishers
Herengracht 370-372
1016 CH Amsterdam
PO Box 323
1000 AH Amsterdam
The Netherlands
T +31 (0)20 524 75 60
F +31 (0)20 524 75 57
bis@bispublishers.nl
www.bispublishers.nl

ISBN 978-90-6369-146-2

Authors: Igor Byttebier, Ramon Vullings, Godelieve Spaas
Design: Vanessa Paterson
Editing: Michele Hutchison, Jane Bemont
Illustrations: Dennis Luijer
Photos: Kathleen Steegmans

Printed in Singapore

CONTENTS

indicates insight pages
indicates training pages

DEAR READER AND CREATOR,

Welcome to Creativity Today...

This is your book if you would like to generate new ideas more easily or if you are looking for tools and techniques to enrich your ideas further. Or is your purpose to coach creative sessions with groups or to apply creativity in organisations? In these pages you will find a hands-on approach for these activities too. It is all here for you, now!

Creativity Today is the international version of the book that marvelled tens of thousands of managers, teachers and students in The Netherlands and Belgium. In no time Creativity Today became the standard by which others are measured. It has facilitated breakthroughs in business and education alike.

Creativity Today is clear, practical, fun and rich with twenty years of experience. It will be your personal creativity coach, bringing you ideas, exercises and inspiration. You will be encouraged to grasp the essence, to put into practice what you've learned and to inspire others. Creativity Today will bring you all the answers to your challenges TODAY.

Igor Byttebier & Ramon Vullings

... and Welcome to Creation Today

Creation Today invites you to envision organisations and organisational development at a deeper level of awareness. How do organisations evolve when we know that reality changes every instant? How will we create new organisations tomorrow?

Through seven organisational cases you will follow the line of thinking, feeling and acting of new leaders of change. You will learn to discover implicit processes in your own organisation and how to use inspiration, co-creation and experimentation as energisers for change.

Creation Today appeals to your responsibility as the creator of your own reality and invites you to apply your newly gained insights to your own organisational environment.

Godelieve Spaas & Igor Byttebier

today:

Don't think this is only a beer coaster. This product has proved itself to comfort human beings in their daily struggle for a better life. It has already been used as:

- ☐ table equalizer
- ☐ message board
- ☐ love letter
- ☐ beamer lifter
- ☐ badge

- ☐ stress reduction tool
- ☐ calculator
- ☐ noise protection system
- ☐ idea thrower
- ☐

If you have discovered more functions of this incredible piece of board, please leave your message at www.newshoestoday.com/beercoaster.

www.newshoestoday.com

CHAPTER ONE
UNDERSTANDING CREATIVITY

THE FIVE MOST IMPORTANT MISCONCEPTIONS

Why is it that after so many years of research and application in the field of creativity, the most crucial insights still haven't reached the greater part of the population? One of the reasons could be that schools don't consider creativity to be a subject worth emphasising. After reading this book, you will probably agree with us that the following misconceptions need to be addressed with greatest urgency.

Misconception 1: 'You're either creative or you're not! You can't learn it.'
Creativity can be learned. Creativity is a skill. Like any skill, some people are endowed with a greater natural talent than others. This is the case with languages or mathematics, balance, memory, etc. It also applies to creativity.

Just as you can improve your basic level in all these skills by actively working on them, so can you improve your creative skills. In this book you will find lots of exercises that will offer you the opportunity to enhance your present creativity skills. Our aim is for you to develop the necessary confidence to be able to find a solution to every single problem you come across. Remember that for every problem there are always several solutions and it is possible to turn problems into opportunities.

Misconception 2: 'Creativity is batik work or flower arranging. It's for softies.'
Creativity has become one of the most important developmental aspects for individuals and organisations. A large number of companies and organisations have discovered that creativity provides the means to bring together both personal and corporate goals. People want interesting jobs. Companies need to change constantly because a status quo can bring complacency. For many years multinationals have offered their employees the opportunity to develop their creative potential within the professional arena. The current trend of accelerated innovation proves it: creativity and result-oriented management go hand in hand. And this is anything but soft.

Misconception 3: 'My boss keeps me from being creative.'

YOU are the only one who decides how to use and develop your creative potential. Obviously, one environment is more stimulating than another but acting the victim has never helped anyone. Consider the obstacles in your environment as a challenge. If your boss doesn't assist you, you have two options: either you help your boss to change, or change bosses.

Do something about your environment. This book will offer you plenty of tips. You can try some of these within your organisation and see what happens. Be bold, but also, be patient: this kind of change takes time. If this doesn't work, find another environment. Many organisations are looking for people who are willing to invest their creative potential in their jobs. And companies (bosses) who refuse to get this message don't have much of a future.

Misconception 4: 'I don't have the time for creativity.'

Creativity doesn't require a lot of time, it requires focus. Of course, we live in a hectic world and we work under pressure – allow this to stimulate your creative potential. Creativity can help you to escape the vicious circle of working in a reactive rather than a proactive way. By asking yourself the right questions about your current way of functioning and managing, new opportunities will arise.

Thinking up new ideas doesn't take a lot of time but it requires focus. Sometimes it is necessary to create some distance from the problem at hand. When you are trained to work creatively, the best ideas will occur to you when you least expect them. Being able to pay close attention to a problem is much more important than having a lot of time.

Misconception 5: 'We already do brainstorming sessions.'

A little learning is a dangerous thing. In many companies people meet for a so-called 'brainstorm'. Often these brainstorming sessions are organised in an unprofessional manner and even the most elementary rules such as 'postponing judgement' are overlooked. These sessions sometimes appear to be based on the shouting out of as many ideas as possible, ideas which nobody really knows how to deal with afterwards. Such performances usually result in a frustrated 'problem owner' as well as frustrated participants. We shouldn't be surprised that the word 'brainstorm' has a negative connotation in many companies.

Some training and a little attention to a number of basic rules can easily enhance the results of these creative sessions. The target should be for the session to render at least twice as many new and useful ideas as a normal meeting would do. *Creativity Today* explains how to achieve this.

IT WAS A DAY LIKE THIS WHEN MARCO POLO LEFT FOR CHINA

WHAT ARE YOUR PLANS FOR TODAY

Loesje

P.O.-BOX 1045 6801 BA ARNHEM
HOLLAND

Welcome to the Work-Out Room!

The training pages are marked with torn edges as shown here. Good luck putting theory into practice.

CREATIVITY TEST

Would you like to test your own current creative ability? This test has no scientific pretensions and doesn't have a scoreboard. The only aim is for you to assess your present creativity, so that you can see for yourself which aspects require attention.

This test is limited to five exercises. You don't have to do them one after the other. Each exercise is accompanied by an explanation of its purpose and indicates the chapter of the book where you can find information on how to enhance a specific skill. Don't feel obliged to take the test right away, if you like you can read further and try it later.

1. Squares: An Exercise in Perception

How many squares do you see here?

Have a close look. Spend two minutes counting the squares, then write down the total. When you have finished, go to page 227 and read the comment.

2. Caesar and Cleopatra: A Briefing and a Question

In a book written by a successful crime novelist we found the following passage which we will use as our briefing. The protagonist is speaking.

> 'I entered the room and immediately I saw the open window, the broken glass and the water on the floor. The curtains in front of the window were moving, but what struck me most were Caesar and Cleopatra. They were both lying on their sides on the floor, in the midst of water and broken glass. It was obvious – they were dead!'

Our question to you: What could be the cause of death? Play the role of the detective and imagine as many causes of death as possible. Use your imagination. When finished, go to page 227 and read the comment.

3. Queues at the Checkout: Reformulating the Problem

This is a true anecdote about a well-known Dutch supermarket chain (Albert Heijn). Several years ago the company organised a customer satisfaction survey. Eighty percent of the customers declared themselves irritated because they had to wait 'such a long time' at the checkout. Of course the marketing people took this result seriously and examined the cause.

They learned that customers had an average waiting time of five to ten minutes, with peaks from 4 pm onwards and on Saturdays. They also noticed that people had the impression they were waiting longer than they actually were. The survey showed that different means of payment (cash, cheque, credit card, etc.) had little influence on the waiting time.

The marketing department organised a brainstorming session to solve this problem. In a brainstorming session, the way a problem is formulated at the outset is very important because this determines the way the solution(s) will be approached.

How would you reformulate the problem of waiting time in the supermarket? Try to come up with several starting formulations. You don't need to look for solutions at this point. This exercise is meant to help you look at the problem from different angles and work out different ways of formulating it. A good starting formulation for a creative session starts with *How can we...*
For instance: How can we better spread the flow of customers at the checkouts? Write down your ideas and then go to page 228 and discover the starting formulation the company chose for their brainstorming session.

4. Organising a Successful Brainstorm: Checklist

Suppose you want to organise a brainstorming session with a group of friends or colleagues to deal with a problem or an issue that has been bothering you for a while and for which no solution has been found. Of course you want to get the most out of this brainstorm. You want to generate creative results and have the group leave the session with a feeling of satisfaction.

Which elements should you pay attention to? What can go wrong? Write down the success factors for a good brainstorm. For creative session coaching tips see page 51.

5. Your Own Creative Resources

Do you know how you generate new ideas? Do you have your own routines to help you when you get stuck? What are you good at? And what are your creative resources? It is worthwhile thinking about these things.

If you experience any difficulty in coming up with answers to the above questions, it might help to look at the new ideas you have recently come up with and think of how these ideas came into existence.

I open my eyes, I accept the world.
I see opportunities and situations I'm willing to change.
I create joyfully and instantly.
I act in connection with the world.
I create my life here and now.
We create our world today.

Igor Byttebier

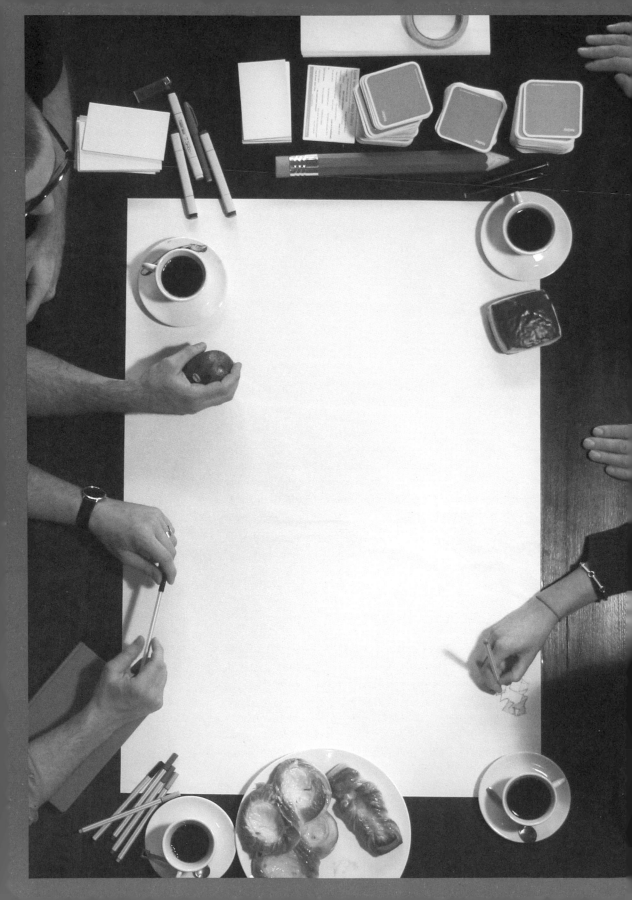

CHAPTER TWO
A CREATIVE MIND

HUMAN THOUGHT

This chapter will provide an insight into our thought processes. We'll have a look at the hardware and software of our thought system. We know that thinking mainly takes place in the brain. But what exactly is thinking? And why don't we constantly come up with new ideas? Do the construction and design of the brain provide an explanation for this? And of course, what is creative thinking?

Definitions

During the course of evolution, man developed a remarkable thought system with an incredibly fine and diverse structure. We will come to the physical aspect (hardware) of the brain in a minute. First let's take a look at the functionality (software). To start with, let's look at some definitions. This is worthwhile because it indicates perfectly why creative thinking is not as simple as we might wish it to be.

What is thinking? Out of many possible definitions, we chose this one:

Thinking = Processing Information

We are constantly surrounded by all kinds of stimuli and our perception system (the senses) makes it possible to capture these stimuli. Our thought system enables us to process very simple but also very complex information. Simple things might be: making a cup of coffee, lacing up your shoes, listening to the weather forecast and choosing suitable clothing. It becomes more complex when we consider the working environment where tasks might be accountancy, political decision making, developing an educational pro-gramme, solving a mathematical problem, repairing an engine, and so on.

An efficient thought system is able to process this complex information quickly and correctly. How do we manage this? By being champions in recog-nising, using and, if necessary, adapting our thought patterns.

What are thought patterns? Thought patterns are clusters of *data* that we recognise as clusters and that we will store if and when they generate *success*. In a comparable situation, we can quickly retrieve these patterns and apply them again. Eventually, this occurs automatically so that we can focus our attention on new or more important problems. Thought patterns are the habits of our thinking.

Experience is the sum of all the patterns and habits we have acquired in the past that make us able to act efficiently and effectively in a certain context.

A simple example clarifies this.

Nina, a Dutch girl, is taking driving lessons: a very complex activity. She already knows how to handle the steering wheel, but now she also has to consider the other traffic, the road signs, the pedals, the gear lever, all of the dashboard instruments and on top of that a thunderstorm spoils her first lesson!

But Nina likes driving and she practises a lot. After a few months she recognises the different road signs, she feels exactly when to shift into a higher gear, she intuitively estimates the right distance between her own car and others and almost subconsciously keeps an eye on the rear view mirror to check the traffic behind her.

She is now able to have conversations, listen to the radio or concentrate on an audio language course. She even solves marketing problems and she has noticed that her best ideas often occur while she's driving on the motorway.

So you're the owner of this fantastic thinking system that enables you to learn fast due to the stability of these rapidly acquired patterns. As a child you learned very simple things first: how to walk, how to sit on a chair without falling off. You learned to read and write letters of the alphabet and consequently you learned how to turn these into words and sentences. But you also learned how to cross the street in a safe way, how you could get your father to do something for you or how to pester your brother or sister without getting punished.

When something is not working you'll try another way. If after a while it does work (this means: if your method is successful), you will remember and apply it again and again until it becomes a habit. A habit is something you do without consciously thinking about it, like brushing your teeth in the morning. It happens 'automatically'. That gives you the opportunity to focus your attention on new things you are learning.

"Creativity is athletics of the mind

Igor Byttebier

You build up experience with a number of successful patterns of thought and action that you have made your own. Experience helps you in your job, in solving difficult problems like tuning a machine, in continuing to teach a class of restless teenagers in a fascinating way, in analysing figures and statistics, in quickly finishing a pile of household chores.

You can do all of this so quickly and efficiently because your thought system recognises successful patterns, remembers them and offers them up ready to use at the right moment. What a wonderful instrument, this thinking machine!

> However, there is also an important flip side.
> Nina is travelling in Scotland with friends. They have hired a local car that has its steering wheel on the 'wrong' side (Nina is used to Dutch cars where the steering wheel is on the left side). When she's driving and wants to shift gears, she grabs for the door handle instead. The indicators are also on the other side of the wheel so that every once in a while she sets the windscreen wipers in action.
>
> Not all the acquired patterns from home are useful in Scotland. But if she pays attention, she learns fast. The journey is fun.

It is quite obvious that a thought system which derives its strength from a stability of patterns and habits by definition must have difficulties in breaking with these patterns and habits. **So pattern-breaking thinking (or creative thinking) isn't treated in a preferential way by nature.** Furthermore, traditional education has historically given this kind of thinking almost no attention compared to other aspects of thought. Coming up with something new is often secondary to acquiring knowledge and training the student in logical pattern-based thinking.

Yet creative thinking is a compendium of skills and techniques that we can learn just as we learned to calculate, to ride a bicycle or to speak a foreign language. The emphasis in creative thinking is on thinking up new solutions, making original links between things, discovering new opportunities. And in learning how to recognise when and where creative thinking can be useful in our jobs, in our personal development, in our daily lives.

Try this: You take three empty cups and ten peanuts. Put all the peanuts in the cups in such a way that you have an odd number of peanuts in each cup. (page 229)

Let's first see if these patterns can also be found in the physical structure of
our brain.

The Human Brain

Our brain consists of 100 to 125 billion neurons and an even larger number
of supporting cells (gliacells). A neuron has a fascinating form. Think of it as
a little ball (the cellular body) with antennae forming entrances and exits.
The entrances are thin, cordlike branches called dendrites. One neuron can
have up to 10,000 dendrites. The exit cord, of which there is only one, is
called an axon. The dendrites receive information from neighbouring cells
and pass them on to the cellular body. A new signal can be initiated from
the cellular body and passed on to other cells through the axon. Axons vary
in length. The shortest ones only reach a neighbouring cell; the longest ones
go from the brain into the spinal marrow and are 20,000 times longer than
the cellular body itself. At its end, the axon splits into smaller antennae that
pass the signal to the dendrites of other cells.

   The signals (each a combination of an electric and a chemical signal) are
transmitted through the neurons which form a jungle of thousands of antennae
interconnected in thousands of ways. Someone has calculated that there are
100 billion connections in our brain. This is 100,000,000,000,000 connections.
The speed of these signals can reach up to 400 km an hour.

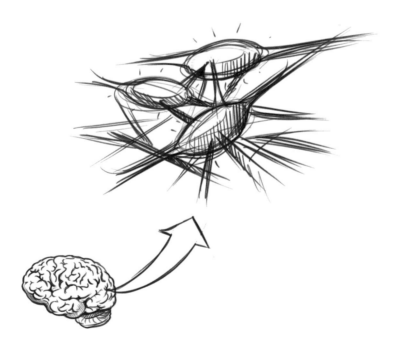

A signal is composed of a combination of various chemical substances (called neurotransmitters), which 'leap' between the cells. The specific combination of quantity and strength of these neurotransmitters gives each signal from one cell to another a 'qualitatively' different flavour. This further enhances the sophistication of communication.

We can only be amazed by the complexity of the brain's structure and it is improbable that humanity will ever get a complete picture of the exact functioning of the human brain. We are certainly not aiming to provide that here; the only purpose of this section is to give you an awareness of the elementary physical basis to our thinking (or our information processing), an understanding of how thought patterns come into existence and the way in which these patterns become naturally dominant.

Which word do the English pronounce as Scottish?

Thinking is about Following Connections and Creating New Ones

Thinking takes place essentially through the transmission of signals between different brain cells and parts of the brain. These signals choose a differentiated path through certain 'circuits'. On one hand, they follow existing tracks, but on the other, they create new connections. Recent research has revealed that only a limited number of new brain cells are added to our brain after birth. However, throughout our entire lives new connections are realised between existing cells in the actively used parts of the brain.

This explains for instance how victims of an accident who suffer from a dysfunction in one part of the brain are able to relearn certain 'lost' functions later on. Other parts of the brain adopt new functions. Specific use changes the physical shape of the brain by 'building' new connections.

In her book *Brainstory*, Susan Greenfield describes the process as follows: 'It seems that the human brain is able to form new connections in order to fulfil an individual's unique needs. It is incredibly flexible and able to learn, to adapt, to improve, and to refine the most frequently used skills, purely as a consequence of stimulation.'

This brings us to the core of how thought patterns are formed: by the brain creating new connections. A pattern becomes permanent because once a connection is established, it is reinforced each time a new signal follows the same trail. Consequently every repeated action increases the probability that the same trail will be followed the next time.

Creative Thinking

Now that you've read about the 'hardware' of patterns and pattern breaking, you'll also understand that pattern breaking occurs by thinking differently. So, thinking differently (use of software) influences the physical structure of the brain (the hardware). How does this going-against-the-pattern thinking work? Let's examine the 'software' of pattern breaking.

Creative thinking is made up of different attitudes, thinking skills and techniques, and thought processes that increase the probability of pattern breaking and the creation of new connections in our brain.

Anybody is able to think creatively: it can be learned and developed. How? Simply by doing it, by practising. As you know, this is the main subject of *Creativity Today*. Just as you can improve your physical fitness by being active and practising sports, you can improve your thinking ability by practising your creative skills.

A few basic creative skills will help you to begin. By training these, you will notice that you already will have improved your ability to think up new solutions, to see different lines of approach, to discover new opportunities. You will also get better at recognising when and where creative thinking will be useful in your job, for your personal development, or in your daily life.

Where do you get your best ideas?

BASIC CREATIVE SKILLS

A number of very elementary skills that constitute the foundation for creative thinking can be distinguished. You already apply each of these skills consciously or unconsciously when you think, act, solve problems, or relax. By improving these basic skills, you will dramatically increase your creative potential. You will also notice that your confidence and motivation will increase as well.

The five basic skills are:
- Creative perception
- Postponing judgement
- Flexible association
- Diverging
- Developing imagination

Each basic skill contributes its own added value to creative thinking and thus to thinking in general. The skills have elements in common and they are interrelated but they can also be distinguished from one another. We have made this distinction for clarity and above all for practise purposes.

Let's start with the skill at the origin of all of our knowledge: perception.

Creative Perception

Scientists have not yet been able to discover exactly how perception functions. We trust our perception in order to explore and interpret the world around us. Through the senses we experience reality. It might even be said that our senses contribute to reality. This means that reality can change when perception changes, an idea that is very important for the creative process, as we will find out later.

Why is a change of perception not that easy? Because already during perception, patterns creep in. Furthermore, often-repeated patterns tend to become more and more dominant.

See how this works by looking at the drawing below. What do you see here? Try to recognise or trace different objects and try to generate different ways of seeing.

When you have come up with five different interpretations of this drawing, go to page 229 and see what the artist intended.

In our society quite a lot of effort (and unintentional effort) is put into influencing our perception of things. Education, advertising and politics each exert their own influence. Equally, reality plays tricks on our creativity by only allowing us to see what there IS. Worse still: we can only see what we THINK is there. So we get 'used' to our own vision of reality. The patterns don't come from the outside; they are firmly rooted in our own perception.

Science has already proved that perception consists of information gathered from outside for only 20%; consequently 80% is produced in the brain itself. This means that we don't see by information coming in so much as by information going out. Rodolfo Llinas, a professor of neurology at the medical faculty of New York University, offers a vigorous defence of the controversial statement that the outside world is a projection created by the brain. 'The only way to understand the huge universe and put it in our little head, is to make internal pictures of the outside world and then check with what is observed.' (*Brainstory*)

Perception, being so elementary, has a direct impact on our thought.
It explains why new visions and concepts need time to break through; they
have to conquer the old visions.

Now, what is creative perception? Creative perception is recognising ten-
dencies and biases in your own perception (and that of others) and setting
yourself free from these. The liberating question is: How can I see this differently? When we learn to observe differently, we are capable of fundamental
innovation. Many changes begin with a new way of looking at things. The
exercise module on page 36 can help to enhance your perceptive capacity.

Postponing Judgement

Judgement is very important. Sharp judgement helps you to safely negotiate
busy traffic. Your judgement helps you to make thousands of minor and
major decisions daily. You learned how to judge as a child. 'You're allowed
to climb onto the chair, but not onto the table.' Later on, you were taught
how to make more complex judgements: in examinations, in conversations, in
dealing with production processes, marketing positioning or strategic choices.

You have probably acquired quite some proficiency in judging. It is hard
to do without it. Judgement directs your thought and actions and you practise
this skill almost constantly.

**There are three levels of judgement, which are not always distinguishable
from one another.**

When you encounter something new, you will first judge if and how this
information 'fits' with what you already know. This is the first level of judgement and it always takes place. This thinking is closely related to recognition.

A sum: You must use the same
digit 3 times in a simple addition
that has 12 as its total. You are
not allowed to use the digit 4.
Which digit can you use then?

"NEVER innovate to compete,

> **Example**
> You walk past two colleagues in the corridor. They are having a conversation and one says to the other: 'What do you think about making our new brochure round, you know, a circular shape?' How well did you hear what he said?

Judgement 1: Generally happens subconsciously. Have I noticed the conversation? Can I place it? Do I understand it?
- You either didn't really hear what he said and you start thinking about something else. End of story
- Or you did hear what he said

At the second level of judgement you decide whether or not to pay attention to the information that you have acquired and to explore it further.
Judgement 2: I explore the new idea. I reflect on it and gauge the consequences. Do I find this information relevant? Is it worth thinking about?
- 'Come on old chap, don't you have anything better to do?' End of story
- Or: 'What do you mean, a circular shape, Alexander? Let's talk about this idea…'

The third level of judgement involves the decision-making after an exploration of the idea. This may be enacted quickly or at length.
Judgement 3: I will use this information/idea, or not. I choose this or I reject it.
- 'Now that we have seriously examined this, Alexander, I don't think we should do it.' End of story
- 'It's actually not that bad an idea, now that we have examined all of the aspects. Ask the graphic designer to come up with something'

Innovative ideas always carry the risk that they will never reach the serious judgement level (judgement 3). Sometimes they are simply not understood (judgement 1); sometimes they are rejected at once (judgement 2). Why is this?
This is because **by definition, new ideas don't fit into existing schemes of thought.** Our brain needs time to get used to a new idea. The idea has to acquire a place for itself within the thought system and that requires time and attention. This means that judgement very often occurs too fast when new ideas are launched. Look at the next page for a short survey of popular 'idea killers'. Undoubtedly you have some you can add yourself.

INNOVATE to change the rules of the game
David O. Adeife

In order to process original ideas (both others and your own) in a sensible way, you will need to develop a more subtle use of judgement. We call this: postponing judgement.

What does postponing judgement mean? When judging a new idea, it is not necessary to fully understand it right away. The art is to be open and accept the idea (by postponing your judgement), even though the idea might not fit into a certain box. By doing so, you create the space in your mind in which the idea's potential can develop. This needn't always require a lot of time. It's more a matter of attitude.

How does this work? The first three activities take place simultaneously. Only then can you start judging.

1. What is meant here? What is this idea?   **Opening**
2. Accept this new thought   **Accepting**
3. Explore the opportunities created by this idea **Exploring**
4. Judge what you are going to do with it   **Judging**

Let's be clear about one thing: postponing judgement does not mean cancelling judgement. In every creative process there is an explicit phase of postponement of judgement. After having explored the potential, we do have to judge the ideas very seriously. There are techniques for this and we will consider them in Chapter Six.

Practising postponement of judgement will also prove beneficial in other aspects of your life. A creative thinker who can easily postpone his judgement will automatically be more open to other opinions, other visions, other cultures. It will be a lot easier for him to explore other opinions without renouncing his own values. It enhances his capacities to discern the various aspects of 'the truth'.

On page 37 you can get to grips with what this creative skill means in practice and you can train your ability to postpone your judgement.

Flexible Association

Let us return for a moment to the structure of the brain, how all of the brain cells are interconnected and continuously transmit signals to one another. The nature of this construction allows for the spontaneous associations to occur.

Association happens when one thought generates another: 'This makes me think of…'

The mention of the words 'weather forecast' might make one think of the television. With association it's almost possible to visualise an impulse travelling via a cable from one cell to another and in doing so, creating its own trail of connections through the brain structure. There are an enormous number of possible paths (via the thousands of dendrites) through the brain structure.

IDEA KILLERS...

Yes, but... It already exists! Our customers won't like that!
WE DON'T HAVE TIME... **NO!** It's not possible...
It's too expensive! Let's be realistic... That's not logical...
We need to do more research... THERE'S NO BUDGET...
I'm not creative... We don't want to make mistakes...
The management won't agree... **GET REAL**...
It's not my responsibility... It's too difficult to master...
THAT'S TOO BIG A CHANGE...
The market is not ready yet... Let's keep it under consideration...
It is just like... **The older generation will not use it...**
WE ARE TOO SMALL FOR THAT...
It might work in other places but not here...
SINCE WHEN ARE YOU THE EXPERT?... That's for the future...
There are no staff members available... **IT IS NOT SUITABLE FOR OUR CLIENTS...**

www.ideakillers.net

Therefore, the word 'milk' can make you think of 'cow', but also of 'white', 'milk bottle', 'coffee', 'baby', and so on.

Nevertheless, some associations are more dominant than others. 'Cow' might have a more obvious association with milk than with 'honey'. In other words, the probability of an impulse leading to the association of 'milk' with 'cow' is higher than its leading to 'honey', unless you have just been talking about 'the land of milk and honey'.

An association with higher odds for realisation is called a 'strong' connection. An association with a lower chance is called a 'weak' connection. If an association (e.g. milk > cow) is repeated several times, it strengthens this pathway and it will grow stronger. This means that the association will occur more quickly and easily in the future. A strong connection has a higher probability of occurring and every time it is repeated, it will be reinforced.

For a frequently repeated thought (e.g. 'What is my sister's new phone number?') our brain will broaden existing connections so that after a while we can carry out this thinking faster. This increase in speed increases the efficiency of thinking and is therefore useful.

At the same time the odds of this association (impulse) choosing another trail in the future become smaller. This is exactly what creative thinking is aiming at. How can we make sure that while looking for alternative solutions (using postponement of judgement) less obvious tracks are explored and/or new connections are realised?

In theory there are two ways to consciously create new connections and we have come up with new terms for them.

'Disociation' or pattern breaking: you avoid an obvious track. The direction of thought deliberately leaves the familiar track.
'Resociation' or linking back: you link from another area of the brain back to a familiar track and make a new connection. The direction of thought proceeds towards the familiar track.

Disociation – Pattern Breaking
Logic will not generate any surprising original thinking. If you follow a riverbed, you know that you will eventually end up in the sea. As a creative thinker you will develop a feeling for recognising fixed patterns as well as the means to escape from these patterns.

Example
Answer the following questions (preferably aloud):
- **What is the colour of snow?**
- **What is the colour of paper in a copier?**
- **A chess set has two kinds of pieces: blacks and...**
- **What does a cow drink?**

Resociation – Linking Back

When you make an new link between an element that does not naturally belong with the subject matter and an element that does, you are linking back. A creative thinker will develop the skill to realise these less obvious connections.

> As an example, a joke:
> Two fish are in a tank, one says to the other:
> 'I'll drive, you man the guns'

Flexible association covers a range of associative thinking skills that can be used by the creative thinker on many occasions during the creative process. Disociation aims at discovering existing patterns and finding new exits. Resociation helps to discover and establish less obvious connections that could solve your problem in a totally original manner. You can become very competent in both skills by training yourself. You will find training material on page 40. And as you have probably already understood: humour is a wonderful resource.

Diverging

The first ideas we come up with, the first thoughts that arise, are based on common sense. This is due to the way the brain is structured and how thought functions (see above). And this is good.

We think with efficiency and concision. When searching for a solution to a problem we tend to stop when we have found a reasonable solution. It also means that if we want to generate new ideas, we will have to think beyond this 'logic'. How? By consciously thinking up more ideas than we would do spontaneously. This means switching off our spontaneous tendency to stop when a common-sense solution has been arrived at, and continuing to come up with ideas. This is called 'diverging'.

How does diverging enhance your creativity? Because when diverging, you automatically reach the limits of what you can spontaneously think of and go beyond them. At that point lies the interesting material, the pattern-breaking new ideas. Remember: by definition, your new ideas don't fit into your existing thought patterns!

Diverging uses all the basic creative skills: speed of association, creative perception, disociation and resociation, finding new tracks, imagining new viewpoints. The basic reflex, 'How could this be done in another way?' guides the creative thinker. He rejects remarks like, 'There is only one solution.' His experience has taught him that there are always other solutions to be found and he knows and trusts that sooner or later a better solution will come up.

If you would like to check your current competence in diverging, go to page 43 for a series of exercises. Chapter Five is completely dedicated to the diverging phase of the creative process and provides creative techniques that will help you to diverge.

Developing Your Imagination

Visual languages are generally less respected than verbal language. School education strongly emphasises the language of words. The consequences of this policy can be found in companies and organisations where we very often notice a lack of visually imaginative skills. Managers are often very capable of outlining a solution but they can't attach an image to it, let alone conceptualise one. Yet, the ability to visualise may be the most important basic skill in the creative thinker's toolbox: no creative solution, simple as it may be, can be thought of, designed and realised without using imagery.

We use the word 'imagination' to refer to the capacity to represent in the mind something that cannot be seen at that moment. We are not only talking about visual images but also about sound, smell, taste and touch as well as abstract notions such as ideas and concepts etc. We can '*imag*'-ine these things. We are able to construct an image.

We use imagination at countless moments in daily life, consciously and unconsciously. We estimate whether we can get a large cupboard through a doorway or not. We prepare ourselves for an interview by imagining it beforehand. We dream in images. We can fantasise: 'When I close my eyes, I am in Honolulu.'

Sheriff John Timber arrived in town on Friday, stayed for three nights and left town on Sunday morning. Please explain.

What is so particular about imagery and why is it so important and useful for creative thinking?

Memory Power – A Fabulous Database

We experience only a very limited part of reality through language. Much of our memory is stored in images. The memory exercise in the training module will convince you of the phenomenal image database you have at your disposal. In traditional education, imagination tends to be neglected resulting in its under-use. By enhancing our imaginative skills we can learn to make better use of this fantastic information resource.

Information Processing Power

The imagination works more holistically and is faster than verbal language.
A picture is a thousand words: this expression nicely sums up the limits of
linguistics. During the creative process, new ideas can be more efficiently
explored and designed using images rather than words. Images force us
to be clear when 'modelling' the imagined reality.

It is common knowledge that Einstein used to do 'fantasy exercises' every
day. He imagined what it would be like to whizz through space on a beam of
light (at the speed of light) and then he imagined a ray of light entering that
cabin of his. This prompted his first vision of the theory of relativity. In creative sessions, participants are stimulated to express new ideas as concretely
as possible, preferably using images to do so.

Emotional Power

When working with images, you're always close to your emotions. Images
reach directly into your emotional world. Remember the image of 'the iron
curtain' that symbolised the distance between capitalism and communism
for decades due to its emotional power. This emotional side is very important for the creative process.

'Some people take no mental
exercise apart from jumping
to conclusions.' Harold Acton

Power of Desire

Imagination of a desired reality, a possible future, a potential new product,
exerts a strong mental attraction. It generates energy. Aristotle said, 'A vivid
image forces the body to realise it.' In top sports, for instance, a vivid image
of a perfect performance helps the body to accomplish that performance.
Mohammed Ali (Cassius Clay), acclaimed as the best sportsman of the past
century, was a fervent 'imaginer'.

Communicative Power

Images have a strong communicative power. During the process of innovation, images and metaphors can prove very powerful instruments of change.
A visionary image of the future can act as a magnet and an engine. President
John Kennedy inspired and stimulated hundreds of researchers at the beginning of the 1960s with his vision of a man walking on the moon.

**Now we understand why imaginative power is of crucial importance to
the creative thinker.** The development of this skill acts as a catalyst in all
innovative processes. People use it to imagine future products, to develop
new visions, to refine primary ideas and to judge ideas more easily.

You might now think about how often you hear managers talk utter non-
sense about a new idea or proposal and realise that they didn't imagine how
the idea would look once it was executed, remaining stuck at the verbal level.
It is more than worthwhile to turn to page 44 and try out some exercises to
improve your imagination.

PRACTISING YOUR CREATIVE SKILLS

Athletes know that they perform better when their basic fitness is optimal. Basic fitness is a preliminary requirement but how about heartbeat, flexibility and reflexes? All athletes use a set of basic training exercises to reach and maintain their level.

The same can be applied to creative thinking. A top-level creative thinker regularly trains the basic fitness of his brain. He can do this by practising a number of basic skills – elementary thought processes which could be considered the raw materials of more complex thinking.

The basic skills for creative thinking are:
- creative perception
- postponing judgement
- flexible association
- diverging
- developing imagination

The following exercises have the same effect on the mind as stretching does on the body. They let your brain know that you are on the case. You can either do the exercises now or try them later on. Don't forget that top creativity is not only about talent and technique but also about practise.

You are probably already good at some of these skills; others may be buried under a layer of dust and some are probably new to you. The different skills influence and strengthen each other. You might be more attracted to the skills you already excel in but you stand to gain the most by developing the skills you find more difficult.

This training section offers exercises on two different levels:
Exercises ! are intended to check if you have understood the exercise, if you execute it in the right manner, and to test your level.

The exercises ask you to generate ideas. Once you've done the exercise and come up with an x number of ideas you are at a good basic level. If you then double (!) the number of ideas (you will find out how hard it is at first) then you are on the advanced level.

Exercises !!! take you to an Olympic level. They dig deeper and require more time. They take you into real life situations. These exercises require more commitment but the greater rewards will undoubtedly compensate for the investment. The **Exercises !!!** show how creative thinking works for real.

The universal rule for all of the exercises is take them at your own pace and continue only as long as you are enjoying it. You can invite friends or colleagues to practise with you and this can provide extra motivation.

Creative Perception

Why? When you observe, you see what is there. Fortunately! But others also see what is there. Observing 'differently' can be the first step towards the creation of something new.

How? You can learn to question your own perceptions (and those of others) while you are observing. You become conscious of your own thought patterns, of the thought patterns of others, but also of the patterns in the way objects (in reality) show themselves to us. The purpose of creative perception is to let go of the dominant perception and become proficient in shifts in perception. This is not an easy task: just try to see a glass as something other than a glass, a magazine as different from a magazine, a company, a consumer, a market, a book…

Question: When was the last time you did something for the first time?

Exercises !

Look at the figure below. What could be represented here? Find as many different interpretations of the image as possible.

Choose an object within hand's reach: a pen for instance, the bedside lamp, the chair you're sitting in, this book. Choose something that appeals to you, preferably a simple and familiar object. Try to develop another vision of this object through changes in perception or differences in interpretation. What else could this be used for or turned into?

Perception is not just visual. Start concentrating now on your other senses; you will be astonished by how much information you can take in. Put *Creativity Today* aside for a moment and concentrate on the following senses one by one:

Hearing – Try to listen to everything that you can hear and make a list. It is interesting to notice how many sounds you normally spontaneously filter away, which you will notice now when concentrating.

Smell – Take a short walk and focus on smell until you have clearly recognised five different scents.

Touch – Pick up *Creativity Today* again, close your eyes and feel each plane of the book until you have perceived something new about it.

Exercises !!!
Look for a room that you can make completely dark, pitch-black. You will find that this is more difficult than you might expect. The best place is probably a cellar or some kind of storeroom. Invite some people to explore the room in the dark with you. Discuss this experience together. Of course you can do this exercise alone as well.

Select one particular customer or group of customers. Conjure up this customer in your imagination and write down their distinguishing characteristics. Now, think some more and seek out their less obvious features until some surprising new visions surface. See if these new perceptions help you to discover new opportunities in your co-operation with this (group of) customer(s).

Postponing Judgement
Why? When you judge, the exploratory thought stage is brought to an end. New ideas are no longer given a chance to surface. By regularly practising postponement of judgement, you will become more open to new ideas, different viewpoints, surprising angles of approach.

How? Postponing judgement is a skill which you can only learn by practice. You have to turn a switch in your head, so to speak, the switch which allows you to postpone your judgement in position A and judge efficiently in position B. A trained creative thinker is able to switch easily from one attitude to the other.

Exercises !

Take your favourite object in the room and make a list of as many disadvantages this object has as you can think of.

Write down the 5 most common prejudices Christians have towards Muslims.

Write down the 5 most common prejudices Muslims have towards Christians.

Do the same for mutual prejudices between the younger and older generations.

Exercises !!!

Listen to the news on the radio and concentrate on the various news items. Choose one and try to look at this subject from the viewpoint of at least 3 different parties involved.

Choose a concrete product or person that irritates you for one reason or another in certain situations (for instance, the lawn mower that makes too much noise; your partner who is almost always later home from work than he/she promised). Think of some positive aspects (advantages) that result from this situation or imagine the way you could turn the situation to your advantage.

Choose your favourite product, your favourite TV programme, or something you like very much. Now think negative thoughts about this product and write down as many disadvantages to it as possible. Go beyond logic. Use each of these disadvantages to create an improvement to your product. This technique, called 'Inverted Brainstorm', is often used for product development.

Think about this for a moment:

> " MADE IN CHINA
> becomes
> CREATED IN CHINA
> Michael Keane

A Real-life Example: DUXON

Corne is a Belgian company that produces packaging material, like the paper used for packaging cheese and meat products in shops. This is a simple and cheap paper product with a transparent polyethylene film glued to the inside in order to maintain hygiene and increase the shelf life of the packaged food.

During a creativity exercise, our company was asked to look for new ideas for this product. We applied the inverted brainstorm technique and came up with countless things that could possibly be wrong with the paper.

We found the product 'a little boring, too square-shaped, it had only one print on it, etc.' This brought us several new ideas about how to enhance the paper, giving it 'a round shape, other colours, an attractive print…'

Then someone said, 'When I come home from the butcher's, I feel like sampling the gorgeous Parma ham. The first package I open contains the salami, the next one is the cheese, then the chicken, and so on. And of course, I only find the delicious ham when I open the very last package. It would be nice if I could find the ham immediately.'

And this was how Duxon came into being; it was the first packaging paper in its category to have a small window showing what is inside. This product was awarded a Packaging Oscar a few years ago.

Sometimes it is really that simple.

Flexible Association

Why? Fast and flexible associative thinking is useful during brainstorming. Association exercises can act as a warm-up and get the brain 'in the mood for creativity'. You can do these exercises individually or in a group.

How? Associations arise spontaneously but you can improve your performance by:

- increasing your speed
- toppling (disociation)
- linking back (resociation)
- connecting

Exercises !

An associative chain is a series of associations where you start with one term and freely associate, always postponing judgement as you move from one association to the next.

Example
water – drinking – soft drink – summer – beach – sailing – surfing...

Exercise in Speed

Use a blank page and start a chain beginning with 'mushroom'. Let your mind wander and do this for 1 minute. Then count the number of associations.

Repeat the exercise. Take a word at random from page 42 and write down another associative chain for 1 minute. Try to increase your total of associations by 50% compared to the previous attempt.

Toppling (chain associations with an extra assignment)

'Toppling' during associative thinking means switching contexts as much as possible. A 'bank' can be a financial company, but it can also be a riverside or a data bank.

An example of switching contexts during an associative chain:
Water – drowning – drunk – pink elephants – circus – artist – Warhol – New York – apple...

Start again with 'mushroom', but try to switch the context as much as you can in your chain.

Do the same exercise, but make associations inspired by all 5 senses.

Linking Back
Start with the word 'Japan' and make a chain that ends with 'mushroom'.

Try to make another 5 chains between Japan and mushroom.

Connecting
Example
What do a sunflower and a fried egg have in common?

sunflower   fried egg

yellow colour

each has a particular smell

Sunday decoration

sunny side up

sunny colour and shape

cheerfulness

a round centre and surrounding material

both taste delicious

nice for kids

the farm...

Find as many similarities (or connecting associations) as possible between:

arena and chips

tea cup and train wagon

All jokes contain a 'tipping point'. Think of a few jokes and find the 'switch' moment in them.
- What is purple and has two white stripes running across it?
- I don't know.
- A tomato wearing braces (suspenders)…
- You said purple!
- Yes but the braces are rather tight.

Exercises !!!
Look to your right and focus on the first reddish object you see and think up 20 different associations around this object.

On the next page you will find a 'value landscape'. Put 3 to 5 suitable values to each of the following:
- the Apple iPod
- your national railway company
- the pop group U2
- the organisation you work in

PLAYFUL	INNOVATIVE	NATURE	TRADITIONAL
INTELLIGENT	POSITIVE	FRESH	SENSITIVITY
CHARISMATIC	REBELLIOUS	MALICIOUS	UNIQUE
PROGRESSIVE	RADIANT	DELIGHT	EXOTIC
TRENDSETTER	HONESTY	REAL	ADVENTURE
FAMILY	STATELY	SECURITY	USABILITY
INDEPENDENT	REPRESENTATIVE	VARIATION	HUMAN EMOTION
GLITTER	HELPFUL	WARM	FOR THE KICKS
ACCESSIBLE	MODERN	STIMULATING	SURPRISE
OLD FASHIONED	CERTAINTY	ONE OF THE FAMILY	COMPASSION
ORIGINAL	SELF-DEVELOPMENT	PROGRESSIVE	INTEGRITY
RELIABLE	LUXURY	COMFORT	LEISURE
SOLIDARITY	OPENNESS	GLAMOUR	DARING
ENERGY	CONTEMPORARY	CLOSENESS	SPONTANEOUS
SENSATION	BALANCED	TENSION	COMMITTED
INTERNATIONAL	QUALITY	HUMOUR	AUTHENTICITY
LIVELY	RESPECTFUL	NON-COMMITTAL	DYNAMIC
HAPPY	REFRESHING	RECOGNIZABILITY	TRUSTWORTHY
COSINESS	EXPERT	CERTAINTY	DECADENT
COOL	POPULAR	CREATIVE	SPIRITUAL
LOVING	SAFETY	SATIRE	TOUCHING

If you like, you can make a distinction between the way the organisation sees itself (the way it would like to be perceived), and the way you think the outside world perceives it. If you think other values fit better into your case study, you can of course add these.

Which are the first 5 brands you spontaneously think of?

What associations do you have with each of these brands?

This is a deep one: How does propaganda work?

What topic is currently hot news and has begun to seem like propaganda in the way that the same associations are constantly repeated?

Diverging

What about today?

Why? The first ideas you think of are generally the most obvious ones. When you continue to diverge (find alternatives), you automatically come up against your own thought barriers. Beyond these barriers lies originality.

How? See how many answers you can find spontaneously to a question or a problem. Try to double this number. It may look like a lot but be confident. With some effort and by using creative thinking techniques, this will turn out to be a piece of cake. Important: of course you must **postpone judgement** while diverging. Otherwise the following exercises would be impossible!

Exercises !
Which of the following letters is different from the others and why?

A E I F U

Do you achieve the results you would like? Go to page 230 to read the comment.

What is 8 divided by 2 (8/2=)?
Give as many answers as you can to this question. We don't provide answers but you can find a helpful technique to try out on page 85, the technique of presuppositions.

Exercises !!!
For each of the following exercises, it is essential to imagine a very concrete situation!

Your best friend will celebrate his/her birthday soon. Think of an original way to surprise him/her in a way that will benefit your friendship.

You want to convince your boss of a brilliant idea although you suspect that he/she will not easily agree. How will you go about this?

If your boss always appreciates your ideas (you're in a minority!), then do the exercise above with a particular customer in mind.

You have to park your car (or bike) for half a day in an area that is known to be unsafe. You fear that it might be gone when you return. Think of an original way to reduce the odds that thieves will steal your car (bike).

Developing Your Imagination

Why? Images are very powerful constructions that are not easily transformed. Yet you can't achieve anything new without creating a new supporting image for it (even unconsciously). Imagining involves making new images as well as letting go of existing ones.

How? Paying close attention and doing simple exercises will help you to become aware of the gold mine of images you have acquired since birth. With a little concentration you can easily access them and start playing with the images you have retrieved.

Exercises !

Let's use our various senses.

- Choose a Coldplay tune or another pop song and let it play in your head. Try to hear as many instruments as possible. Concentrate on details
- Can you hear the sound of a crowd in a soccer stadium going mad after the winning goal?
- Can you taste a fresh pint of beer, or a glass of dry white wine, while enjoying the sun in Provence in France?
- Can you imagine the feel of velvet or the hair of your beloved?
- Can you smell a freshly mowed lawn, or a delicious cup of coffee?
- Can you picture Neo, struggling through the crowd, in the movie The Matrix? Or E.T. pointing his finger?
- Choose another movie that you haven't seen for the past 5 years and try to retrieve as many images as you can

Can you hear the clocks?

Pick up an object that is within your reach now. Look at it attentively, taking in as many details as possible during one full minute. Then put the object aside, close your eyes and try to imagine it again. Try to retrieve all of the details. It can helpful to do this exercise with two people. The other person can interrogate you about the object.

People will **accept** your ideas
much more readily if you tell them
Benjamin Franklin said it first
David H. Comins

Remember a classroom from your childhood associated with happy memories. Retrieve it from your memory and try to construct a clear and detailed view in your mind. Which teacher do you see in front of the classroom? Who is sitting next to you? What did the walls look like? And the furniture?

The purpose of this exercise is not to visualise an image that completely matches reality, but to create a clear, sharp view with a lot of details. You will notice that after a few minutes, details you had 'forgotten' will pop up again.

Exercises !!!

Let's see if you can take a better look at your working environment just by using your imagination. Close your eyes and imagine your workplace. Look at the details, walk around, touch the furniture. What do you see? What do you hear?

Now ask yourself the question, what disturbs or irritates you? Look around in your imagination and take mental note of it. Then in your imagination adapt what you would like to change. Change everything you want, postponing your judgement, and be surprised at the results.

Choose a product (or service) that you have to deal with in your own work and that you are quite pleased with. Imagine this product (or service).

Now try to change a number of elements in your imagination. Change the colour, enlarge or reduce parts, change their positioning or order. Give them a new use. Delete some elements and see what happens...

Do this without a specific goal in mind, just as an imagination exercise. This technique (called 'SCAMPER') will also be treated in Chapter Six, page 147.

POSTPONING JUDGEMENT

NOT...

MARC: Eric, what would you think about selling all our trucks and just concentrating on the rest of our business?

ERIC: Haha, you must be kidding, a haulier without trucks! Never heard of it. You'd better not tell this to our boss. Forget about it, lad. Can't you think of anything better?

BUT MAYBE...

MARC: Eric, what would you think about selling all our trucks and just concentrating on the rest of our business?

ERIC: What do you mean, Marc? I don't get it. Can you explain it to me?

MARC: Well, I know that our company has grown thanks to our transport business. But if you take a close look at the cost structure, most of our capital is going to these trucks while our profit margins continue to drop. If we didn't own the trucks, we could use that money for other activities that would allow larger profit margins.

ERIC: Yes, I think I understand what you mean. What activities are you thinking of?

MARC: I don't know exactly. Maybe we could help customers find the best way of transport or routing, or we could help other hauliers optimise the costs, or maybe there are other possibilities. I'm sure we can think of more ideas.

ERIC: We could think of opportunities in other branches, for instance increasing the safety of transport, optimising environmental costs, the training of truck drivers... It seems worthwhile to think about this further and have a look at the figures.

MARC: Yes, and if it proves to have potential, we can propose it to the boss.

ERIC: We'll have to think about how to propose this, you know he's very sensitive when it comes to his trucks.

CHAPTER THREE
THE CREATIVE PROCESS

Models or diagrams help us to get a grip on reality which is often too complex for our comprehension. There are hundreds of ways to express creative processes, from the depictions of a genius' brainwave to the endlessly detailed flow chart of an engineering project. This book offers a very simple general format that will hopefully inspire you by its simplicity.

Some people find it highly inappropriate to try to capture creativity in models. 'How can one even try and catch the elusive in a structure?' However, you will see that some models can be very useful for understanding and steering the creative processes. They help you to direct your thinking and to concentrate on those elements of the creative process where you can make a difference. It works as long as we don't take the models for reality.

The most simple form of the creative process consists of three phases:
- Starting phase   Chapter Four
- Diverging phase   Chapter Five
- Converging phase   Chapter Six

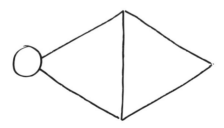

There is no need to tackle the chapters chronologically. See for yourself what you find interesting or new. Go ahead and experiment. By entering the creative process, you will automatically come across those aspects that follow your learning needs: 'The proof of the pudding is in the eating!'

Starting Phase

The starting phase – as you have already guessed – indicates that the process starts one way or another. Perhaps there is a problem to solve or you are confronted with some kind of assignment or task. Perhaps you have discovered an opportunity, or something in your work or private life irritates you. Or you might just be trying to make changes.

Within a company, changing circumstances may result in the need to approach the business differently. The change might be that the organisation must become more customer-oriented. Or that the market for traditional products is becoming saturated. A joint venture creates new opportunities. A move towards the stock exchange generates the need to consider the aspirations of the stockholders. You wish to introduce a fantastic new product onto the market. You want an original web design, etc. All these different kinds of situations can trigger the creative process.

The above situations are treated in Chapter Four. You will learn how to recognise opportunities and problems, how to formulate your goal in order to obtain an optimal creative result and how to recognise the difference between problems that are best handled with creativity and others that are not.

Make this equation work by changing only one character: 5 + 5 + 5 = 550 (and > or < is not what we are looking for)

Diverging Phase

Once you have set off in the right direction, you can move on to the diverging phase. For novices in the field of creative thought, Chapter Five will prove to be the most surprising one. Creative techniques will help you to generate new ideas beyond your wildest expectations. Some techniques are closely related to logical thinking and use a reasoning technique to break patterns. Some require the use of associative and imaginative skills. A third type will teach you how to trust your intuition and show that you are always surrounded with solutions to your problem once you have found the right state of mind.

Converging Phase

In the third stage an abundance of ideas forces you to make choices. Many people who are already familiar with creative thinking have noticed that once you can successfully apply diverging techniques, the biggest challenge in the creative process is not generating new ideas but the next step: the converging phase. How do you transform an abundance of ideas into the best solution? How do you design concepts quickly and efficiently? How do you increase the speed in which innovative concepts are implemented? The techniques and methods in Chapter Six will provide you with answers to the above questions.

TIPS FOR THE COACH

Creative Session

In the following three chapters we will offer you practical tips for coaching groups through the creative process. This book will not turn you into an expert creativity coach. You can only acquire expertise by practising and building on experience. Still, these practical tips will help you to set off in the right direction.

You will find tips in text boxes like this one. They apply to the specific phase of the creative process in the appropriate module. Both tips for starters and for more experienced creativity coaches are included. Of course, it is always a good idea to read through *Creativity Today* again later, once you have gained more experience.

The questions below will be treated in the following chapters so that you can turn a creative session into a successful experience for all parties concerned.

Problem Is the problem clear enough and is it a problem to which creativity can provide a solution? Does the formulation need to be reworked before the brainstorming session?

Problem Owner Have you located the right problem owner? Does he really want to solve the problem and is he capable of doing so? Can he give a good briefing?

Composition of the Group How many people do you invite and who do you choose? Does your group consist not only of specialists but also some 'wild geese'?

Environment Is the space for the brainstorming session suitable? Does it have enough daylight and fresh air? Can you concentrate easily? Is it an inspiring place? Do you have a flip chart? Can you stick sheets of paper on the walls?

Timing Did you plan enough time, but not too much? Have you written a script including all the different steps? Is there someone to help you to keep time?

Coach Who will lead the session? Have you appointed a particular person? Hopefully not the problem owner?

Techniques How do you get the group 'in the mood'? Do you have some warming-up exercises to start with? Which diverging techniques are you going to use and how much time do they require? In what manner do you plan to converge?

Closing How will you conclude the brainstorm and how can you increase the odds that the ideas generated will be realised? Will you keep the group informed of the results?

I have a dream...

I say to you today, my friends, so even though we face the difficulties of today and tomorrow, I still have a dream. It is a dream deeply rooted in the American dream.

I have a dream that one day this nation will rise up and live out the true meaning of its creed: 'We hold these truths to be self-evident: that all men are created equal.'

I have a dream that one day on the red hills of Georgia the sons of former slaves and the sons of former slave owners will be able to sit down together at the table of brotherhood.

I have a dream that one day even the state of Mississippi, a state sweltering with the heat of injustice, sweltering with the heat of oppression, will be transformed into an oasis of freedom and justice.

I have a dream that my four little children will one day live in a nation where they will not be judged by the colour of their skin but by the content of their character.

I have a dream today.

Martin Luther King

CREATIVE PROCESS

A model/diagram describes the creative process as seen from a rational, content-oriented approach. This of course doesn't contain the whole truth; other elements are equally important to the success of creative achievement: emotion, energy, enthusiasm.

In this respect you could also conceive the creative process as two cyclones which follow one another.

During the **starting phase** you will look at all the items on the ground and analyse them. Everything is structured and organised. You know that the creative cyclone will pass very soon. You fasten a number of items down so that they won't move. Others are left loose to be moved and swept at random by the cyclone.

Diverging. The cyclone passes, a whirlwind of thoughts blows across the area, sweeping away old structures to make space for new opportunities. The wind blows in all directions. It blows in gusts, sometimes hard, sometimes soft. Everything that has not been fastened down whirls around and is carried very high up into the air.

After a while, the first cyclone loses its power and gravity starts to take effect again. A new, downwards whirling movement emerges. All floating elements are attracted towards the ground by this reverse cyclone. The elements are composed in a new manner, brought into focus and set back down on the ground.

The **converging phase** ends here with us looking at the 'renewed' structure. This phase is about understanding the new logic, fixing down some elements, gently rearranging others, making the place look spic and span and announcing to the public that the new visitors are welcome on the premises.

This is one way in which we can conceive the sensory and 'sensational' side of the creative process. However, any comparison is bound to fail and different people experience the creative process in very different ways.

Use Your New Understanding of the Creative Process to Solve Your Own Problems and Open up Opportunities!

You will get more out of *Creativity Today* if you practise using your own problems and opportunities while reading this book. Whilst learning more about creativity you can solve some of your own problems at the same time.

Write down a few topics you would like to (or need to) address in the coaster boxes on the next page. Later on in *Creativity Today* we will return to the topics on that page.

The important thing is that you have to experience creativity to really understand what it is all about. That's why we dedicate so much attention in the training modules to all kinds of experiences and perceptions.

What kind of feelings can you expect to experience in the following chapters?
- restlessness while trying to obtain a clear problem formulation
- feeling of anticipation during the first round of ideas
- sinking feeling when finding yourself stuck in your own thought patterns
- doubting being able to find a better idea
- sense of freedom due to unlimited diverging
- release when new insights occur
- energy when you finally get to the action
- astonishment at the results of your own creative power
- tension when choosing which ideas are the best
- being in full flow when things work seamlessly
- eagerness to come up with your most promising concepts
- enthusiasm at working with others
- fear of failure when presenting your most favourite ideas
- pride when looking back at the final results

RIGHT! AND NOW ON TO THE STARTING PHASE!

CREATIVITY
seems to be a rather pompous word for the work I have to do between now and next Tuesday

David Ogilvy

CHAPTER FOUR
THE STARTING PHASE

STARTING AND GETTING STARTED

When does the creative process start? Well, there is starting and getting started. Sometimes you have already taken off before you actually realise it. In fact you are constantly thinking up solutions and putting them into practice. You get stuck in a traffic jam so you find an alternative route to your destination. The dog ate your daughter's doll and you try to find a way to comfort her. You quite like this new young lady or young man you meet at the company party and you're thinking about a 'suitable' opening line. The starting phase can be a very natural process without much deliberate thought.

On other occasions you are positively determined to find new solutions to a specific problem or you need to find new ways to deal with a situation. The stimulus to come up with new ideas can originate *from yourself*. You're doing something new or you have new targets, or perhaps you are dissatisfied with the way things are going at the moment.

Sometimes your environment can trigger a creative process. Your husband, your wife or your children, your boss, your customers want something different. And you're the one who has to come up with the ideas.

You might be confronted with something that catches your attention. It appeals to you. The thought 'Why isn't this different?' occurs to you or you think, 'I could do this better.' A detail catches your eye and you want to do something about it.

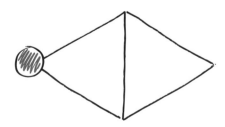

PROBLEMS AND OPPORTUNITIES

Creativity is often associated with problem solving but the creative process also allows you to discover opportunities and to benefit from them. What exactly is the difference? What is a problem? And when is it an opportunity?

Problems

You have a problem when:

1. you're *not satisfied* with the current situation, and
2. you don't have an immediate answer to *how* you can improve the situation

The second part of this definition makes the distinction between a problem and a task. You have to deal with lots of problematic situations but most of these can be seen as task-led. You know the different steps that will lead to finding a solution. You tackle the task and solve the problem. By tomorrow there will be another pile of tasks waiting for you at the office: customers needing a quote, a report you have to write...

The first part of the definition indicates that a problem arises from a feeling of dissatisfaction with the current situation. One sometimes defines a problem as the difference between the existing and the desired situation. The feeling of dissatisfaction generates the necessary energy to tackle the problem and to solve it. Creativity can help you in this.

Opportunities

However, the opposite is also true: without dissatisfaction we are less inclined to improve existing situations. This could be called 'the problem of not having a problem'.

But there's more. Remember the way in which we observe things in set patterns (see page 23). We take the existing situation for granted without even noticing that the 'here and now' can be improved. Yet we are constantly surrounded by opportunities. An opportunity can only exist if somebody can see it. So many opportunities are lost just because we are not aware of them.

ASKING THE RIGHT QUESTION

Example

A good real-life example about problems and opportunities took place a few years ago in the Dutch harbour of Scheveningen. There is a fishing fleet there, part of which specialises in cod fishing. Now, you should know that cod fishing is undertaken in teams of two boats dragging a net of about a hundred metres long. These teams, often made up of relatives, put out to sea together and once they have reached their location, they fix the net between the two boats, pull it until it's full and then haul it in. The cod is carried on the two boats alternatively, per trip. The whole thing is a delicate operation which requires precision on the high seas.

John and Peter, the captains of the two boats, planned to go fishing together on a certain day. Unfortunately, John had to be taken to hospital the night before for an appendix operation and so the fishing couldn't take place. John had a problem that the doctor could solve but Peter also had a problem, he had lost his fishing mate.

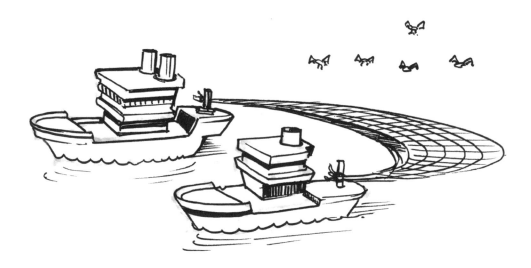

S HALF THE RIGHT ANSWER

anonymous

Peter thought up some creative, alternative solutions and finally put one of them into practice. Could you repeat his thinking? What ideas can you come up with? What would you do if you were in Peter's situation? Try to think of some solutions first, after that you can turn to page 231 to see what Peter eventually did.

Opportunity Scouting

From John and Peter's story we learn that we are constantly surrounded by opportunities. So why wait until problems arise? You can also start scouting for opportunities immediately.

The investigation or discovery of 'hidden' opportunities is an important skill in a fast changing world and has become crucial for every organisation. It is an attitude, a disposition, but you can also turn scouting for opportunities into a process. You can train yourself in this from page 69 onwards. For the time being, we will stick to the useful notion that both problems and opportunities can stimulate your creativity.

STARTING CONSCIOUSLY

In certain situations it is useful to take a closer look at the starting phase. This proves useful when the subject is complex or if you don't know exactly what you want to obtain. Particularly in a professional context or if you want to assemble a creative group to tackle a problem, it is rewarding to consider the starting phase with care. Well begun is half done.

Using the exploration circle (see next page), you can explore the subject from three angles: feel, think and want. 'Think' refers to a number of analytical questions about the subject. Finally you can define your starting formulation and move on to the diverging phase.

The following pages in this module are rather technical and fast-paced for beginners. Feel free to skip this part and jump to the next module on page 69. If you want to gain an insight into the subtleties of and models for the application of the creative process within organisations right now, then continue here.

The Exploration Circle

At the start of the creative process you should ask questions about yourself, about the subject, and about your relation to the subject. Sometimes this questioning is intuitive and unstructured and this is sufficient. However, it is generally more useful to spend more time taking a closer look. The exploration circle provides a good checklist for this 'digging'.

The circle helps you consider the problem from three angles: feel, think and want. You can apply the circle within a team, a department, or the company. The organisation is also an entity that feels (has its own culture), thinks (gathers and processes knowledge) and wants (makes strategic choices).

THE EXPLORATION CIRCLE

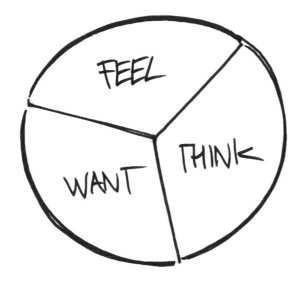

Feel – considers what you feel about the subject NOW and your relation to it
- How do I feel at this very moment? Do I feel comfortable with myself?
- Do I have time for this subject?
- Am I in a creative mood?
- How do I feel in relation to the topic?
- Do I feel like going for it? Will it be energising?

Think – mainly concerns the subject
- Do we have all of the information?
- Who is the problem owner?
- Do we have enough time?
- Is it a suitable topic for creativity?
- What is the underlying goal?

Want – mainly concerns yourself and the future
- Do I (do we) want to invest energy in this? What are our aims?
- Does this fit with the global image, with what we want to achieve overall?
- How important is it? Is it a priority?
- Will we, as soon as we have the results, immediately go into action?
- Do I feel comfortable with these activities?

These three elements of the exploration circle might seem very self-evident. Yet we often notice that at least one of the elements of the circle has not been carefully considered before the creative process gets started. This is often due to the culture of the organisation putting too much emphasis on one of the three aspects and consequently overlooking the others.

Feel: In many companies, 'feeling' is an underestimated aspect of management. Nevertheless a creative process will seldom be successfully concluded when the 'feeling' is missing. Very often your feelings for the subject will grow during the creative process. On the other hand, there is absolutely no sense in investing a lot of energy in a subject that doesn't really interest you. Why would you? There are enough other topics about.

TIP FOR THE COACH

HOW DO YOU DO A 'FEELING CHECK' WITH A GROUP? YOU SIMPLY GO FROM ONE PERSON TO ANOTHER AND ASK FOR EVERYONE'S FEELINGS ON THE SUBJECT. EVERYBODY SHOULD HAVE THE CHANCE TO EXPRESS A FEELING, WHILE POSTPONING JUDGEMENT. NOBODY IS RESPONSIBLE FOR WHAT THEY FEEL AT A GIVEN MOMENT. THIS MEASURING OF FEELINGS CAN GIVE YOU AS A COACH AN INDICATION OF HOW BEST TO APPROACH THE SUBJECT DURING THE CREATIVE PROCESS.

Think: Some groups (or individuals) allow their feelings to dominate too much. They forget the common sense of asking a number of concrete and precise questions about the subject and the environment. Not focusing sufficiently on the analytical aspect reduces the quality of the creative process. Sometimes it also causes unrealistic expectations and, consequently, disappointment.

Want: Sometimes we notice a lack of focus. People want to achieve many different things and preferably all at the same time. They are not able to prioritise. The consequence is chaos and many 'broken dreams'.

It is vital for the quality of your creative process to check that you're not going to waste your time and energy on a subject that generates little motivation. If this is the case, you may come up with some reasonable ideas but these will not really change the situation.

A Suitable Subject for Creativity?

Creativity is a fashionable word which managers and politicians like to use. A common belief is that creativity is able to solve any problem but this is simply not the case. Some problems require different kinds of solutions, not creative ones. Disappointment is the logical consequence of situations where creative processes are not correctly applied and unrealistic expectations are built up.

It isn't very easy to judge whether or not creativity can make the difference. The following questions may help to distinguish appropriate subjects.

Do we need new ideas for this subject? Will new ideas make a difference here, or do we need a different kind of approach? In order to avoid misunderstandings, we want to make it clear that creativity can at least contribute to finding solutions, but not always to the same extent.

New ideas do not make a difference:
- If we don't fully understand the subject (through a lack of crucial information, or if it is too complex)
- If we estimate that the subject is not important enough, or we don't really want to tackle it (lack of motivation)
- If the ideas already exist but we are unable to make a choice (insufficient information)
- If the ideas already exist but we are not in a position to make a choice (lack of authority)
- If the ideas already exist but we don't dare to make a choice (lack of leadership)
- If the path to a solution is already clear, but we don't want to suffer the consequences yet (lack of vision and/or motivation)
- If the solution is already obvious, but we are not able to realise it (lack of competence and/or authority)

Persistent problems usually combine some of the above elements. Take the problem of traffic jams, for instance. A simple analysis will show you that this is not a creativity problem (as is nevertheless often claimed). Hundreds of ideas exist already but a real solution requires the political courage and competence to take the necessary decisions, as well as the social motivation to go through the inevitable difficult period of implementation.

Therefore what is sometimes missing is not new ideas but the necessary:
Vision to explore future possibilities and 'imagine' the improved reality.
Information to understand the circumstances or to make concrete choices.
Motivation to tackle the problem.
Courage to make necessary but unpleasant decisions.
Competence to lead a complex process to a satisfactory result.

In all of these situations, creativity can only solve part of the problem and other instruments are required for the rest.

Analytical Questions
Which are the most logical, and yet often forgotten, analytical questions you should ask during the starting phase of the creative process?

Is the Subject Clear? Have We Asked the Right Question(s)?
A problem may seem very clear until you ask a few concrete questions, at which point it suddenly seems to topple. Upon further analysis a technical problem may become a commercial problem, or an apparently simple and obvious problem may be the cover for a jungle of complexities, as occurs in situations concerning political manoeuvres, for instance.

By reformulating the problem you can find out how clear the issue is and if the problem really is the problem.

Do We Have Access to the Relevant Data?
Valuable time is lost when important information is not or not immediately available when analysing the issue. This has two negative effects:
- Due to the lack of information, the wrong problem might be tackled
- After the diverging phase it will be difficult to make choices because it is not possible to decide which ideas will really solve the problem

This kind of failure is commonly encountered in product development. A company sees a need for new products. A creative team thinks up new ideas and then it suddenly becomes clear that nobody is able to decide on the best concepts because they don't really know what the customer wants.

What can you do about this? You should ask yourself beforehand what kind of information is necessary to really understand this problem to its full extent. Gather that information and have it available during the starting phase. If this is not possible, you can consider postponing the starting phase until the information is actually available. One of the most crucial pieces of information is: Who is the problem owner?

Who is the Problem Owner?
Creative processes often go wrong (even in well-known companies and at higher management levels) for the simple reason that it is not clear who the owner of the problem is. A real problem owner is concerned, committed, competent and capable (4C's).
Concerned: He is (emotionally) involved with the problem. It means something to him.
Committed: This is a step further than concerned. He is willing to tackle and solve the problem. He will take action as soon as good ideas surface.

Competent: He is authorised to tackle the problem, he can formally and informally deal with this problem, he is qualified to make decisions and act accordingly.

Capable: He has the necessary capacities and skills to tackle the problem (decisiveness, personal authority, budget, etc.).

What can go wrong?
- Sometimes a person (or department) whom you expect to want to solve the problem might have reasons not to go the whole way. In this case they are qualified, but not committed
- Sometimes a person (or department) lacks the right capacities. In this case they are committed and competent, but not capable
- Sometimes they may be committed and capable but not decisive enough and they may not have the authority to deal with the problem properly

Before you organise a creative session where the problem owner will brief everyone about their problem, it is always useful to check that you have located the right problem owner.

Example

During a three-day creativity course in a company that produces building materials we came across an interesting production problem. In the final stage of a coating process, small latent flaws would occur on some coated roofing tiles that had just emerged from the coating machines. Two engineers had been searching for an elegant and inexpensive solution to this problem for several weeks.

The two engineers briefed the creativity group. We thought of dozens of possible solutions, some of which were very useful. After the brainstorming session, to our astonishment, the problem owners considered none of the solutions to be promising.

We discovered later that something else was at stake here. Imagine a creative group finding a solution in just two hours to a problem that the two of you had spent weeks on without result. This doesn't look good, does it?

The two engineers were definitely concerned, competent and capable but not committed to implementing our solutions.

Do We Have Enough Time to Deal with This Problem?

On the one hand this might seem an obvious remark. On the other hand we notice that companies still tend to consider creativity and innovation as something that can be done in between 'normal' activities: brainstorms during lunchtime, concept development after hours.

Do make sure that the time available is sufficient for the creative process to provide good quality results. A little pressure is acceptable and keeps the mind sharp, deadlines help us to focus and to converge the different elements. However, a creative process also needs enough time to give a good quality result.

The Starting Formulation

You should end this phase with the starting formulation for the diverging phase. After having checked your feelings about the matter at hand, analysed the issue, and considered your motivation, you are ready to think up new ideas. What is the best way to formulate your goal at the beginning of the diverging phase? A number of simple rules can help you.

State the Goal in One Sentence

Many managers have difficulty explaining the essence of a problem in clear and concise terms. The 'one sentence rule' helps them. Furthermore it forces you all to make a choice about how to approach the problem.

Don't Formulate in Broad or General Terms but Maintain a Concrete Focus

If you state your problem on too high an abstract level, you will generate general and uninspiring solutions.

> **Example**
> 'How can we solve the problem of traffic jams?' is a very broad statement. You might formulate more concretely by focusing on, for example, 'the traffic problem on the M25 during the morning rush hour'. Even more concrete: 'How can we encourage car-pooling during the morning rush hour on the M25?' Or 'How do we avoid having 'single-person-vehicles' on the M25 during morning rush hours?'

A problem may often be divided into several partial problems. It is better to then deal with the partial problems separately or to tackle the most striking problem first.

'If you give away everything you have, you are left with nothing. This forces you to look, to be aware, to replenish.' Paul Arden

> **Example**
> 'How can we increase the profit margin on product X?' can be divided into:
> - How can we buy in more cheaply?
> - How can we reduce the costs of selling?
> - How can we increase the output of the production process?
> - How can we create added value for product X for this particular target group?
> - How can we create an alternative distribution system (in order to reduce costs and increase efficiency)?

Mention the Problem Owner in the Formulation

You read a definition of the problem owner above. Some problems have several owners. For example: How can South London companies and governmental organisations contribute to car-pooling during rush hour on the M25?

A Question that Starts with 'HOW' or 'CREATE' Invites New Ideas

The interrogatives Who, What, Where, When, Why invite the gathering of information. They should be answered during the briefing. In order to invite people to think up solutions for your particular objective, the best way to commence your starting formulation is: **How can we... or Create (Design/ Come up with)...**

The How question focuses on the way you want to accomplish something. **The Create phrase (or Design/Come up with)** focuses on the final result.

> **Examples**
> How can we halve the number of traffic victims over three years?
> Create a great slogan for a new lawn mower.
> Create a book concept where the reader writes the book himself.
> Design an original pen for teenagers.

Find a Challenging and Attractive Formulation for Your Goal

A challenging and attractive formulation generates the energy and enthusiasm a group needs to reach the goal.
'How can we increase the sales of product X by 20%?'
'How can we make at least half of our customers wildly excited about our new product X?' is more rousing than: 'How can we sell more of product X?'

TIPS FOR THE COACH

Creative Session
As a creativity coach, how do you organise the starting phase of a creative session?

Beforehand Run through the above questions concerning the problem and the problem owner. You can go through the briefing with the problem owner. Invite the creative group and organise a room and a time slot.

Group Composition A creative group should consist of 4 to 12 participants. The number can vary according to the objectives. A diverse composition is very important. An ideal creative group has the following make up:

1/3 specialists on the problem
1/3 generalists
1/3 wild geese

The term 'wild geese' means people you invite not just because they are creative, but also and more importantly because they know little or nothing about the subject. They don't have fixed thought patterns and will not be limited by them during the diverging phase. Often this group is not represented at brainstorm sessions, which always leads to a loss of quality.

Creative Room A good environment for a creative session is spacious, uncluttered and has both daylight and fresh air. All the material you will need as a coach should be on hand. Preferably you will choose a space outside the working environment.

Timing The time you'll need can vary quite a bit but a few hours is really the minimum. As a coach you will have drawn up a mini-scenario indicating the amount of time allocated to the various phases and techniques.

Creative Session, Starting Phase
- Welcome
- Refresher on the brainstorming rules (see page 83), and warming-up exercises
- Briefing: The problem owner explains the problem
- The group asks questions, if necessary using the circle of exploration
- Reformulation: Each participant establishes his own starting formulation
- This is discussed in the group
- Choice of one starting formulation as a kick-off for the diverging phase
- Start of the diverging phase

STARTING PHASE

The Starter's Frame of Mind

Why? At the start of the creative process you want to prepare yourself for a top creative performance. You let go of everything you were doing before and start to focus your attention on the here and now. You condition your body and mind for a strong performance. This preparation time will result in better results later on.

How? There are no general rules. Everyone has their own way, maybe even a ritual to get into the mood. Do you prefer working to a deadline or not, with or without music, in a separate space or not, a quiet room or a busy environment? Are you an early bird or a night-time person? Do you perform better in a group or on your own?

Exercises !

Find out how you like to get started. Either consciously or subconsciously you will have developed some methods for this. You will certainly increase the future pay off by spending a little extra attention on this aspect of the process.

Make your own CD with music that puts you in a creative mood.

Exercises !!!

You will find a number of warm-up exercises below which can help to set up a creative mood in a group:
- Do some association exercises with the group (see page 40), possibly linked with the theme of the briefing. Write these on a flip chart
- Perception exercises make you aware of thought patterns. You can find suitable pictures on the Internet
- You might have asked the participants beforehand to bring a favourite object to the session. Let them talk about it
- Ask them to do an original drawing. For example: draw an original zoo, dog, fruit tree… Don't make it too difficult. Let people explain what they have done
- You ask the group to stand up and get into a circle. Send a gesture around the circle. The person who starts makes a specific physical movement, the second person copies the movement, changes something and passes it on to the next person, and so on
- Let the participants talk about an occasion when they have been a big spender, focusing on an object or an activity which they spent way too much money on and which they are still a little ashamed of, or on the contrary, very proud of
- Do 'fitness-in-the-airplane' exercises
- Ask people to tell the group who their hero is, and why

- 'How would you like to be remembered by your colleagues once you have left this organisation?'
- Have a humorous brainstorm on a playful subject

Of course it is even better to come up with your own warm-up exercises. Adapt them to your own style and to the subject the creative session is about.

Scouting for Opportunities

Why? Problems arise. You don't have to make any special effort to find them. You will have to look for opportunities yourself. Once you have started you will notice you are surrounded by opportunities; they are out there just waiting to be found.

How? First you must develop an opportunity-sensitive attitude: look at your environment with an open, fresh mind as if you are seeing it for the first time; let what you see astonish you. Then start looking for opportunities, and don't forget to postpone judgement during the first phase.

Exercises !

Read the magazine article below. Who (which person or organisation) could derive opportunities from this situation? Think of 5 opportunities, then go to page 232. You may have come up with some of these ideas yourself.

> **Animal Doctors**
>
> We regularly come across articles about dogs that protect or rescue their masters. We also know that dogs are sometimes used to locate wounded people.
>
> It is less known, however, that pets can also help with diagnosing and curing people. Her mistress has a terrible headache and can't sleep, Puss jumps on the bed, licks the painful neck and the headache disappears. Katie the Dog often accompanies her owner when she visits patients in a hospital. At first Sophie, a depressed lady in a psychiatric ward, doesn't accept Katie but Katie keeps pushing her wet nose against Sophie's hand until she starts stroking her. Then Sophie begins to talk to her. A moment later she has recounted her life story. In that one hour she has talked more than she has done during the past six weeks.
>
> The behaviour of this cat and dog fits into the social repertoire of pets; it has also been observed with dolphins, parrots and wolves who take care of sick or wounded fellows. They share body warmth, helping the wounded animal to conserve energy and as a result strengthen the social ties within the group.

Pick up a magazine or a newspaper and choose an article about a subject that you find interesting but which you don't have to know a lot about. Scout for some opportunities for the concerned parties or for those not directly concerned, or for yourself, your family, friends, company…

Exercises !!!
(It is easier if you don't do these **Exercises !!!** on your own. In a small group people can help each other to cross initial thought barriers.)

Think of new products or services you could provide, relating to the scenario of the hundreds of thousands of people who spend time in traffic jams every morning, listening to the radio, picking their noses, gazing at other people and getting tired.

Put on a pair of metaphorical opportunity glasses and walk around for about ten minutes in your living room or work environment. Try to consider your surroundings with a fresh view and think up a few opportunities to improve it, postponing judgement. At first, you will be reminded of some of those features that disturbed you previously. Move on until you come up with opportunities that you hadn't noticed before.

Take the organisation that you currently work for (or another one if you prefer) as a starting point. Pick up a newspaper or a magazine and thumb through it. Scout for opportunities for the chosen organisation. Let yourself be inspired by everything you find in the newspaper or the magazine. 'Diverge' while remembering postponement of judgement.

> Are you **stupid** enough to solve the problem?
> (Creativity doesn't come from **knowledge**, judgement does)
> Willem Stortelder

The Starting Formulation
Why? A correct and clear formulation of a problem or an opportunity provides the optimal starting point for the diverging phase of the creative process. The starting formulation describes the target, the objective you want to accomplish. Reformulation generates different viewpoints.
   Reformulating is especially useful in a group process since it increases the commitment of every participant, avoids misunderstandings, generates new viewpoints and results in a shared final formulation.

How? See page 66 for a number of rules to obtain a good starting formulation.

Exercises !

Vanessa just finished studying to be a medical secretary. Before she starts looking for a job, she wants to travel but she has little money for that. On top of that she knows that her parents won't be very happy when they hear about her plans for a world tour.

Write down 5 starting formulations for Vanessa in this situation and choose the one you think is the most relevant. When you have finished, turn to page 232 for a few examples.

A good friend of yours has a couple of adolescents at home, at the 'difficult age'. One of her sons is very stubborn, doesn't respect the house rules and constantly talks about moving out. Your friend is particularly concerned that the boy will go astray. Write down around 10 starting formulations that shed light on different aspects of the situation.

Think about subjects that currently are attracting your attention or look on page 55 to see which subjects you wrote down earlier. Choose three of them and come up with around 5 starting formulations for each of your topics. Choose the most inspiring formulation from each list. You can use these formulations to start the exercises of the diverging stage.

Exercises !!!

The complaints department of the supermarket chain Albert Heijn in Holland receives a lot of complaints from customers who feel they have to wait too long at the checkout. In this hectic age people consider this as time wasted (see the elaborate briefing on page 15). What would be a good starting formulation for a creative session? Go to page 228 afterwards and see how Albert Heijn approached this.

The Human Resources department of a manufacturer of domestic appliances is confronted with the problem of having some very experienced staff who seem incapable or unwilling to adapt to new technologies. They also employ a group of younger people who are inexperienced but who have grown up with computers. Collaboration between the two groups is far from brilliant.

'Try again. Fail again. Fail better.' Samuel Beckett

The increasing pace of work causes stress in the first group. These employees do not really want to make any effort to use the new technology available and feel as if the 'progressive youngsters' are forcing them into situations out of their control.

The second group is impatient and ambitious but they would benefit from sharing the experience and support of the older generation in order to grow into the business. Find some starting formulations that could enable you to tackle this problem.

TODAY   CATEGORY *Case studies*

SUBJECT TITLE *Introduction*

DESCRIPTION *Actively apply your own creativity*

BRIEFING

Here and at the end of the following two chapters you'll find a few detailed case studies with this layout which will enable you to experience the creative process in practice. We invite you to tackle these cases in order to find out what a real creativity experience is about.

Don't forget: reading a book on creativity is fun, but it won't make you any more creative. You will only learn by practising!

You attempt three designer case studies and one organisation/company case study. These examples have been chosen so that everyone can benefit from them. You can tackle them on your own or work in a group.

Further on in *Creativity Today* you will find ideas and solutions from others who have already had a go at these examples. In this way the case studies give you the opportunity to practise creative techniques and to assess your solutions afterwards.

GOOD LUCK!

TODAY   CATEGORY Designer case study

SUBJECT TITLE Tables

DESCRIPTION Design original tables

BRIEFING

Tables have been around for millennia and their shape has not fundamentally changed since their conception. This makes them an interesting challenge for a thinking exercise.

Imagine you are a designer in a furniture manufacturing company. An international furniture fair in Milan with a special competition for new table concepts is coming up. This will be an occasion for you to show off your expertise. How do you take up this challenge? Using the diverging techniques on page 118, you can achieve this.

TODAY   CATEGORY Designer case study

SUBJECT TITLE Toothbrushes

DESCRIPTION Invent new toothbrushes

BRIEFING

Teeth-cleaning is a morning and evening ritual for all or most of us. You pick up a toothbrush, open the tube of toothpaste, put toothpaste onto the toothbrush, switch on the cold tap and off you go.

But why can't this be done differently? Brushing is always the same and toothbrushes all look alike.

Can you conceive of new types of toothbrushes and, consequently, new ways of brushing your teeth? This should be possible! The diverging techniques on page 119 will be useful here.

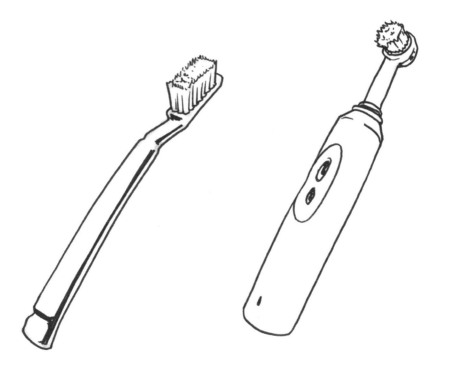

TODAY   CATEGORY Designer case study

SUBJECT TITLE Bridges

DESCRIPTION

Come up with a new concept for a bridge

BRIEFING

Want to think big? Awaken the construction engineer within. It is not easy, but not impossible. Imagine new bridge concepts to span a river of at least 15 metres wide and 5 metres deep. Use the diverging techniques on page 120.

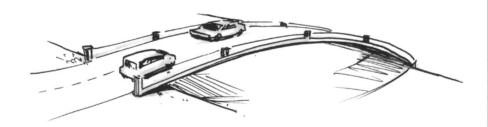

TODAY   CATEGORY Organisation case study

SUBJECT TITLE Railway strike

DESCRIPTION Imagine alternatives

BRIEFING

Contrary to the designer case studies this story is situated in a more detailed context. It is a fictitious case, although not unimaginable.

Strikes are in vogue again. Several economic groups and unions are using this method to obtain higher wages or to fulfil other demands. Strikes still seem the ultimate means to an end. Hasn't anyone thought of an alternative yet?

Ordinary people on the street, the customers of service industries, however, are fed up with being used as hostages in negotiations. Pilots keep airplanes on the ground, trains remain in the station, no mail is delivered, teachers don't teach. (Although we have to admit that the latter are generally then praised by their 'direct customers'.)

Unions should realise that there is an end to the customer's patience and that strikes that deliberately obstruct large groups of the population are also regarded as signs of disrespect to these people.

Let's suppose that we all are the representatives of the (union of) railway guards. Yet another restructuring is being planned at 'National Rail' headquarters and we don't like what we see. Management are planning to reorganise the schedules again so that our working hours and habits will change, holiday planning will be thrown into confusion, wage structure will be jeopardised, and so on. We're all furious. Some hotheads are already talking about a strike that would involve all National Rail train staff.

On the other hand we know that our customers, the average railway passenger, will not appreciate this action. In the current social climate, the strike might work against us.

TODAY   CATEGORY Organisation case study

SUBJECT TITLE Railway strike

DESCRIPTION Imagine alternatives

BRIEFING

Think of one or more activities you could undertake to force the management to withdraw the proposed restructuring and to increase wages in addition. With these activities you should gain the sympathy of the passengers and the general public (or at least not lose it).

How should you tackle this case if you are the coach of a creative session treating this subject? Look at the following questions:

1. Who would you invite to this session? Go to page 68 to read about the ideal composition of a group for a creative session; now compose your group.

2. Which questions should be answered beforehand in order to begin this session well? The circle of exploration and the analytical questions from pages 60 to 64 could be very useful.

3. Can you think of some alternative formulations of the problem? Remember that various definitions offer different views of a problem. Afterwards you can choose the best one.

Now you have all the elements necessary to organise a creative session for this case study. The following chapter provides various diverging techniques that can help you in the diverging stage. Will you be doing this on your own? Or will you invite a couple of friends to practise with you? Both are possible.

The passengers of National Rail are most grateful!

This case has already been treated by a creative group. You can read about their problem formulations and diverging phase on page 121.

'I am just a copier, an impostor. I wait, I read magazines.
After a while my brain sends me a product...
I am my brain's publisher.' Philippe Starck

'I am just a copier, an impostor. I wait, I read magazines.
After a while my brain sends me a product...
I am my brain's publisher.' Philippe Starck

'I am just a copier, an impostor. I wait, I read magazines.
After a while my brain sends me a product...
I am my brain's publisher.' Philippe Starck

'I am just a copier, an impostor. I wait, I read magazines.
After a while my brain sends me a product...
I am my brain's publisher.' Philippe Starck

'I am just a copier, an impostor. I wait, I read magazines.
After a while my brain sends me a product...
I am my brain's publisher.' Philippe Starck

'I am just a copier, an impostor. I wait, I read magazines.
After a while my brain sends me a product...
I am my brain's publisher.' Philippe Starck

'I am just a copier, an impostor. I wait, I read magazines.
After a while my brain sends me a product...
I am my brain's publisher.' Philippe Starck

'I am just a copier, an impostor. I wait, I read magazines.
After a while my brain sends me a product...
I am my brain's publisher.' Philippe Starck

'I am just a copier, an impostor. I wait, I read magazines.
After a while my brain sends me a product...
I am my brain's publisher.' Philippe Starck

'I am just a copier, an impostor. I wait, I read magazines.
After a while my brain sends me a product...
I am my brain's publisher.' Philippe Starck

'I am just a copier, an impostor. I wait, I read magazines.
After a while my brain sends me a product...
I am my brain's publisher.' Philippe Starck

'I am just a copier, an impostor. I wait, I read magazines.
After a while my brain sends me a product...
I am my brain's publisher.' Philippe Starck

'I am just a copier, an impostor. I wait, I read magazines.
After a while my brain sends me a product...
I am my brain's publisher.' Philippe Starck

'I am just a copier, an impostor. I wait, I read magazines.
After a while my brain sends me a product...
I am my brain's publisher.' Philippe Starck

'I am just a copier, an impostor. I wait, I read magazines.
After a while my brain sends me a product...

CHAPTER FIVE
THE DIVERGING PHASE

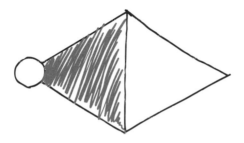

Diverging Towards a Whole Range of Ideas...

Following on from the starting phase in which you analyse the problem, consider it from various angles, and determine the correct starting formulation, you now need to generate new ideas. You move on to the diverging stage; this means trying to find as many new ideas as possible for a given problem or objective. If this is your first introduction to creative thinking, this module will undoubtedly have some surprises in store for you. You will discover seven powerful diverging techniques that guarantee you will never be at a loss for new ideas.

Here we will explore the use of the techniques and the situations in which these techniques work best. There are different ways of working through this chapter.

First Round, Second Round

You can stimulate diverging for yourself and others by creating **a kind of ideation space in the mind with room for fun, experiment and fantasy**. It should be a space where more is possible than in reality and where you are allowed to leave dominant thought paths. Postponing judgement is crucial in the diverging phase.

There are two diverging rounds. **In the first round you should express all the ideas you spontaneously come up with.** These may be simple, common sense ideas but crazy ideas are also welcome. At a certain moment you will reach a threshold when you can't add anything more to the list of ideas. At this point you have reached the limits of your spontaneous imagination.

"**ideas** are like rabbits, You get a **couple** and learn how to handle them and pretty soon you have a **dozen**...

John Steinbeck

TIP FOR THE COACH

'Rules of the Game' for Creative Sessions

The diverging phase should always be played out according to a number of rules in order to create an open mindset within the group.

Postpone judgement. All ideas are welcome. This is the Golden Rule of creativity! Any kind of judgement – including self-criticism – has a paralysing effect on divergence. Remarks such as 'we have already tried this', 'this is technically impossible' or 'too expensive' act as a plug on the creative volcano and mean that some ideas will never be uttered. With the 'postponement of judgement' rule you can give all ideas a chance to grow. All ideas are welcome, logical and illogical, vague and concrete. Consistency is not necessary.

Remember, this is a temporary attitude: there will be judgement, but later in the creative process (see Chapter Six). In other words, generating new ideas and judging them are strictly separated during the creative process.

Foster openness within the creative group. But respect privacy in the outside world. No idea spoken during the diverging phase should go further than the group. Only those topics that have passed the judgement phase can be communicated externally. Until that moment the privacy rule should apply for the whole group of creative thinkers. This creates a greater openness within the group; participants dare to express more and dig deeper.

Pay extra attention to naive ideas. By definition, a new idea doesn't fit with our established thought patterns. An experienced facilitator will therefore pay extra attention to ideas which might not seem immediately applicable. These ideas might contain the breakthrough that the group is looking for.

No hierarchy, no arrogance. Everybody is equal in a creative session. Differences in status, age, gender, experience are not relevant. The group is composed of various kinds of people precisely because that variety increases the quality of the ideas.

Hitchhike on others' ideas. An idea can serve as a stepping stone for other ideas. Pay attention to every idea and don't refrain from taking up others' ideas. A vague idea can be developed further. A wild idea can generate a feasible idea or make a new angle visible. In other words, when somebody else's idea makes you think of a new idea, just express it. And accept at the same time that others can develop your favourite idea.

Next you can start the second round which increases the quantity and inno-vative power of your ideas. Using one or more techniques you will try to break conscious and unconscious thought barriers and discover new perspectives.

Diverging Techniques

Dozens of techniques have been developed in order to support the diverging phase. If you would like to know more please refer to the bibliography at the back. For *Creativity Today* we have made a heterogeneous selection of the most powerful techniques. You can either apply them one by one or combine them, and work individually or in a group.

These techniques are:
- Presuppositions
- Direct analogy
- Superhero
- Personal analogy
- Random stimulation
- Free incubation
- Guided imagery

All diverging techniques make use of two important thinking activities: **estrangement and resociation**. These concepts can be easily visualised. Suppose you're driving on the motorway; you feel a bit bored and you're searching for adventure. You turn off the motorway and begin your journey of discovery. You take side roads and let the environment surprise you, you enjoy yourself and look around, forgetting about the motorway. This is what we call estrangement.

After a while you turn your mind back to your original destination. You want to continue towards your destination without following the same route you are used to. You keep your destination in mind and trust your sense of direction. You find new roads. What you're now doing is called resociation. **Estrangement** means that your conscious attention is no longer focused on the problem or the objective, but you direct your attention towards an element or situation unrelated to the problem. **Resociating** is a conscious thought activity which forces a return from that element or situation towards the problem or objective. In this way, new connections are established in your brain that can lead to new ideas and perspectives.

Most diverging creative techniques use these two types of thinking activities in one way or another. The techniques differ from each other through the way you estrange yourself from the problem. However, you always apply resociation (see also page 110).

Ask yourself: Which of your friends have you never asked to help you out with an assignment

Presuppositions

What are they? Presuppositions are thought patterns that arise automatically when a person reflects on a specific issue. Presuppositions can be instigated by the phrasing or the context of the problem, or they can be related to the thinker's personal experiences or to the wider environment this person belongs to (e.g. company, sector, profession, department, family, school or university, religion, country).

Presuppositions are a natural part of the thought process (see Chapter Two). They are generally very valuable and positive since they regulate our daily lives. They simplify communication and decision-making; when booking an airline ticket for instance, you suppose that an airplane is the faster way to travel, that it has been well maintained and has enough fuel. You also suppose that the pilots will respect the security rules in the air.

Yet presuppositions also set limits to divergence. They represent a specific vision and so prevent you from viewing the problem from another angle. Many useful ideas and trains of thought may remain out of reach. When you succeed in identifying these limiting presuppositions and temporarily eliminating them, you can break your old thought patterns and a useful change of perspective will come about.

Presuppositions may be consciously or unconsciously present. Think of Freddy who wants to launch a promotional campaign for his bakery. One of Freddy's conscious presuppositions is that the campaign is only for his customers and that it shouldn't cost more than 1,000 euros. Freddy also uses a few unconscious presuppositions: his competitors won't participate in this campaign and that it is all about bread.

How does the technique work? The technique consists of allotting time in the diverging phase to the detection of (conscious and unconscious) presuppositions in order to eliminate them temporarily afterwards, while remembering to postpone judgement. There are two basic methods with which to identify presuppositions.

First Method

A. You consider a few crucial terms in the starting formulation.
   For example: Crucial terms in the question 'How can we reduce the queues at the checkout in the supermarket?' are queue, cash desk, reduce.
B. Then you trace the presuppositions that are connected with these words or their context.

Let's take 'QUEUE'.
What are the presuppositions related to this word and to our perception of it?
   1. The customers queue up one behind the other thus forming a line
   2. They have their trolleys with them

3. The first one in line is served first, then the second one and so on
4. They are 'waiting'
5. They are silent etc.

C. After that, you take each presupposition and ask the question:
What if this presupposition didn't apply here, or what if we inverted
the presupposition? What kind of new ideas would arise?

1. Customers don't need to stand one behind the other. This can lead to
the system of numbered tickets where the customer is called when it's
their turn. Or the people don't need to stand in a straight line (but a
snaking queue like you have in amusement parks or airports).
This reduces frustration
2. Customers don't have to wait with their trolleys. They could put the
trolleys in the queue, walk around a little longer and return when it's
their turn. The only thing that remains to be done is to find someone
to push the trolleys forwards
3. There could be a 'surprise line' where the order of service is determined by drawing lots
4. You could ask the customers to help the people in front of them.
This would speed up the process
5. Have the people talk to each other. This could be organised. Is the
line as long as before? Let them talk about how they could reduce it. Etc.

Your turn
Suppose one of your friends is a student at a fashion academy and asks you
to find a new way of organising this year's final fashion show. Use the presupposition techniques and ask yourself which presuppositions you can discover
behind the term 'fashion show'.

Second Method
A. You start with the ideas from the first round.
B. You look at the solutions, detect common characteristics in these ideas
and write them down. These common features are the presuppositions.
C. Then you do exactly as described above, in C.

Your turn
Suppose you're asked to design new table concepts for a modern interior (see
also page 118). You want to do this using the second presupposition method.

A. Start to draw several tables
B. Search the presuppositions all these designs have in common. List them
C. Break them down one by one and think of new concepts

For instance: a table without legs could hang from the ceiling, could be fixed to the wall, could rest on a person's lap, etc. A tabletop doesn't need to be horizontal. A vertical tabletop is conceivable if you, for example, fix drinking glasses to the wall by using Velcro strips on their sides.

Presuppositions
First Method
1. Starting formulation
2. First round
3. Select crucial terms in the starting formulation
4. Determine the presuppositions included in each term
5. For each presupposition, ask the question:
   'What if we eliminate or reverse the presupposition?'
6. Resociate (think of new ideas)

Second Method
1. Starting formulation
2. First round
3. Write down the common characteristics of the first ideas.
   These indicate presuppositions
4. For each presupposition, ask the question:
   'What if we eliminate or reverse the presupposition?'
5. Resociate (think of new ideas)

'High creativity is responding to situations without critical thought... If you want creative workers, give them enough time to play.' John Cleese

TIP FOR THE COACH

Creative Session
The presupposition technique makes one consider one's own thinking; it is therefore sometimes regarded as rather 'difficult'. One also needs to be skilled in postponing judgement. Nevertheless, using presuppositions rapidly leads to new insights and is a good starting technique after the first round of spontaneously generated ideas. The technique is very suitable for organisational and technical problems. When applying this technique in a group you will need participants who are capable of approaching their own thinking in a critical manner. This requires discipline. Because of the emotional involvement, this technique is more difficult to apply when person-oriented or psycho-logical topics are being tackled.

Direct Analogy

What is it? When can you say that two things are analogous? Two elements seem analogous if they have (from our brain's perspective) similar characteristics. These similar characteristics are called 'the analogy base'. We can say that a mug and a glass are analogous because they have a large analogy base, but there are differences too.

Mug

Not transparent
Has a handle
Generally for hot drinks
Usually a more bulky shape
Strong association with coffee,
milk, tea and other hot drink

Glass

Transparent
No handle
Generally for cold drinks
Usually a finer shape
Association with water
and refreshments

Both

Used to drink from
Are hollow
Open on top
Can't leak
Usually have a round shape
Leave rings on the tabletop
Are hand-held

A mug and a glass are considered to be more analogous than for instance a mug and a traffic light because we spontaneously recognise a larger analogy base for the first two elements and because we also consider the analogies to be relevant.

Recognising analogies is a basic quality of the human mind. It is part of the associative thought we use to build up general knowledge. When we observe something new, connections are made in the brain with our existing knowledge (thought patterns). If this weren't so, we wouldn't be able to recognise what is new. (Hence perhaps the word re-'cognise'.)

Remember the first time you saw a 'sitting ball'. It might have taken you a few seconds to make the connection ball – chair. This link (analogy base) is realised by means of the function of the objects: 'sitting'. But there are also important differences, for instance in stability.

We make use of this type of basic human thinking in creative analogy techniques, though in different ways from those used in normal life. With the technique of direct analogy, we try to make surprising connections between an element within the problem context (the subject) and an element outside of the problem context (the 'analogon'). Then we resociate towards new ideas.

How does the technique work? When using direct analogy, you look for inspiration in a theme (or analogon) that is not at all related to the problem. You use this analogon as a starting point from which to resociate towards your starting formulation. How does this work in practise?

A. You choose an analogon that will serve as source of inspiration.
The analogon should meet the following conditions:
- Be a concrete term
- Be far removed from the subject
- Be inspiring

Examples of analogons: countries (China), animals (woodpecker, squid), sports and hobbies (fishing), vehicles (Ferrari), etc. The analogon can be any item that meets the three above criteria.

"Creativity is the power to connect the seemingly unconnected
William Plomer

B. You write down features and associations of this analogon.

To serve as an example, let's use our tables on page 118 and choose an animal as an analogon, an elephant for instance. We start from the specific characteristics of and associations with this analogon.

Table   Elephant

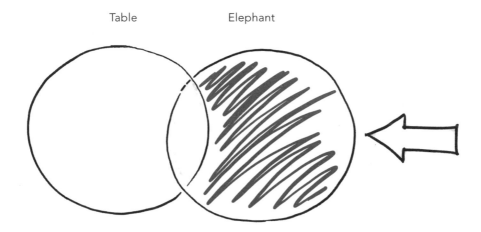

We try to find at least 5 particular characteristics for this analogon.

An elephant
- has a trunk
- lives in a herd
- has a good memory
- comes from Africa or India
- performs in a circus
- has big ears etc.

C. Resociation

For example:
- The 'trunk' could make us think of a kind of built-in vacuum cleaner in the table, to be used to clean the tabletop
- The 'herd' generates the idea of a series of smaller tables that can slide into one another
- A good 'memory': why not insert a horizontal computer screen into the tabletop so that you can browse the morning news on the Internet while you have breakfast?

You will observe that a different kind of ideas is generated here than those which resulted from the presupposition technique. Now you can go further and search for ideas based on the other characteristics of an elephant.

Direct Analogy
1. Starting formulation
2. First round
3. Choose an analogon
4. What is specific to this analogon?
   Write down its characteristics and associations
5. Make every feature a starting point in the search for new ideas.
   Resociate

This technique is sometimes called '**analogy with nature**'. Nature is considered to mean everything that humans are surrounded by and which they are a part of. The idea behind this is that for every single problem, however big or small, nature always offers a solution.

There is even a science called bionics which studies the functioning of organic systems and applies their mechanics to concrete technical problems. Many inventions have their origin in nature: the undercarriage of a fighter jet that has to land on an aircraft carrier is based on the 'hinge joints' in a grasshopper's legs; the surface of Olympic swimsuits is similar to shark skin; the structured surface on the back lights of cars is derived from a dragonfly's wings, for the shape causes mini-turbulence which prevents dust and dirt from becoming attached to the surface.

TIP FOR THE COACH

DIRECT ANALOGY IS A HIGHLY ACCESSIBLE TECHNIQUE WITH A BROAD RANGE OF APPLICATIONS AND MOST GROUPS EXPERIENCE IT AS VERY REWARDING.

A FEW PRACTICAL TIPS: THE ANALOGON SHOULD BE INSPIRING AND SUFFICIENTLY KNOWN IN ORDER TO GENERATE A NUMBER OF PARTICULAR CHARACTERISTICS THAT CAN LEAD TO A FLUENT AND VARIED FLOW OF IDEAS. FROM WHAT IS EXPLAINED ABOVE, WE SEE THAT AN ANALOGON CHOSEN FROM NATURE CAN PROVE TO BE VERY INSPIRING FOR MANY PEOPLE.

Superhero

What is it? As a child you probably admired the ingenuity of Batman, Zorro or Mickey Mouse, always able to find a way of turning desperate situations into something good. The superhero technique brings these heroes back to life in concrete problem situations.

'Superhero' is an example of a fantastical analogy. The fantastical analogy is related to the former technique although, unlike like direct analogy, it isn't limited to reality. We can let our imagination go wild when choosing an analogon. This creates another angle from which to view the problem and from there, new ideas can be generated.

How does the technique work? Think of a hero or a heroine whom you are in awe of, in a positive or negative way. Fairytales, comics, cartoons or science fiction can be a valuable source of inspiration. Always choose a hero or heroine with whom you are well acquainted. It's preferable not to choose stereotypical heroes. Your hero may also be a real or historical person but for the sake of the exercise you will need to raise this person to a mythical status.

Now bring the chosen hero or heroine to life in your thoughts. What does he or she look like? How does she move? What does she feel? What is she capable of? Once you have your heroine in mind, ask yourself how she would react when confronted with the actual problem. How would she tackle this problem? You then transform every solution you find into concrete suggestions for solving the problem.

Examples of heroes or heroines might be: Batman, Leonardo da Vinci, Gandhi, Frodo, Madonna, Lara Croft, Monsieur Poirot, your (late) grandmother, Harry Potter, Philippe Starck, Inspector Morse, David Copperfield, Flipper the dolphin, Andy Warhol, Nelson Mandela, your white blood cells...

How would Leonardo da Vinci handle the queue problem ('How can we create a more pleasant atmosphere during the waiting time at the checkout?' see page 228). His perspective drawing of the Last Supper might make you think of optical illusion: visual tricks could make the waiting line seem shorter or hide it from view. His Mona Lisa could lead you to a philosophical approach towards the whole issue (make the waiting seem worthwhile) or teach people how to paint in the waiting line. His drawings of helicopters could introduce the third dimension. Why not consider putting checkouts on different levels, not only on the ground surface?

On page 113 you can practise with your superheroes.

'Success consists of going from failure to failure without loss of enthusiasm.' Winston Churchill

IMAGINATION
IS MORE IMPORTANT THAN KNOWLEDGE
Albert Einstein

Superhero
1. Starting formulation
2. First round
3. Think of a hero or a heroine
4. Bring the hero or the heroine to life
   Which characteristics could you attribute to him or her?
5. How would the hero or the heroine tackle your problem?
6. Transform the suggestions into concrete solutions for the problem.
   Resociate

A variation on this method is to read a story in which the protagonist encounters several problems. While reading you can pay attention to the solutions proposed in the story. Afterwards, you can try to transform the solutions from the story into solutions for the actual problem.

Fairytales are written in a very expressive language which makes them very useful here. They lead us into a world of wonders and unlimited fantasy. Their structure is remarkably similar to the creative process: there is a problem to be solved, obstacles occur and finally a solution is found. The fantastical solutions that the hero or heroine comes up with can incite you to think up fantastical ideas concerning your own problem. The world is full of fairytales: the tales of Grimm, Andersen, Perrault, Hauff, 1001 nights...

TIP FOR THE COACH

IN GENERAL PEOPLE LIKE THIS TECHNIQUE VERY MUCH. IT IS OBVIOUSLY VERY PLAYFUL AND BRINGS OUT THE CHILD IN US. WHEN APPLYING THIS TECHNIQUE IN A GROUP, LET EVERY PARTICIPANT CHOOSE A DIFFERENT HERO. THIS BRINGS MORE DIVERSITY TO THE FLOW OF IDEAS.

I can't understand why people

Personal Analogy

What is it? This technique grew from the fact that technicians and inventors often seem to identify quite strongly with the object of their attention. A mechanic listens to an engine as if it wants to tell him something. A captain attributes female characteristics to his ship and talks about her as if she had a will of her own. All of us are inclined to speak to (or shout at) our computers when they 'let us down' at critical moments.

The personal analogy technique appeals strongly to the empathy and imagination parts of the psyche. When using this technique, new ideas spring up through the creative's empathy with an OBJECT (not a person) within the problem context. This is not simple but challenging and inspiring.

'Those who lack courage will always find a philosophy to justify it.' Albert Camus

How does the technique work? You select a central object from the problem context and ask yourself: 'How would I feel if I were this object in this particular situation?' You try to experience this feeling of identification as intensely as possible. The degree of empathy is crucial to the success of this technique. Beginning with that feeling, you ask yourself the following question: 'What would I do now (if I were this object with this feeling in this situation)? How would I react or act?' In this imaginary situation you try to work out how the object would react if it were a living being. Then you resociate towards the starting formulation. What new ideas come to mind?

Using personal analogy is a little more complex than the three former techniques. Here are some examples to clarify how it works.

> **Example 1: Become Dough**
> Biscuit manufacturer General Biscuits used this method to solve a problem of overcapacity of a production line. They approached the problem using the question, 'How would I feel if I were the drop of dough introduced into the machine?' It is quite obvious that this requires seeing the machine from an entirely different perspective (in this case from inside!). Doing so will generate new ideas during the creative process.

are frightened of new ideas...

Example 2: Become a Reminder

We discovered another example in a start-up computer company which had problems with defaulters. The problem became so huge that they decided to organise a creative session to tackle the issue. They used the technique of personal analogy, asking the question, 'How would I feel if I were the reminder and arrived on the non-paying customer's desk? What would I try to do then?' One of the reactions was, 'I arrive in the post to the customer's address. However, I never reach the financial director's desk, I get stuck on the secretary's desk. She puts me in a file. I feel small and misunderstood.' These feelings were captured and elaborated upon. The feeling of not being understood lead towards ideas such as: make a reminder-tape that addresses the customer vocally or a talking reminder that catches his attention. The feeling of being small generated the idea of enlarging the reminder: producing a giant reminder that people couldn't ignore, or a reminder with a strange shape that wouldn't fit into the files and thus would continue to draw attention to itself.

Suddenly a new direction of thought appeared. Don't enlarge the size of the reminder, but increase the amount to be paid. Finally, they chose this solution. They sent a reminder to every defaulter and added a zero to the amount due. Result: dozens of phone calls from protesting customers. The reminder had obviously caught their attention. The financial department of this young company had carefully planned this and let the customers know that the amount was 'an error', but that the multiplication by ten symbolised the importance of these due invoices. Some people were startled, others understood the company's actions, many clients paid. Of course, this was clearly a one-shot campaign.

I'm frightened of the old ones"
John Cage

Example 3: Become a Clay Pigeon
And finally, a problem that didn't arise in a professional environment. A group of Australian teenagers built an apparatus for clay pigeon shooting in the common area behind their houses as a bit of summer fun. However, when the pigeons were not hit they landed in the adjacent cornfield. The boys could not retrieve the pigeons without damaging the crops. When the farmer complained to their parents, the clay pigeon shooting was banned. What happened next?

The boys approached the problem from all kinds of logical angles, without success. In the end, they applied personal analogy, 'How would I feel if I were a clay pigeon and the farmer found me in his field; what would I try to do?' A large number of reactions lead to various suggestions. The most illustrative reaction was, 'I would feel guilty and so embarrassed that I would sink into the ground in shame.' The leader of the group then asked the question, 'What kind of clay pigeon would sink into the ground?' The first useful answer was, 'It could be made of pressed and sun-dried clay, so that it would dissolve when it rains.' Next: 'The pigeons could be made of fertilizer, that would please the farmer!'

Finally came the suggestion that they developed: 'Make the pigeons from ice!' The teenagers had some moulds made which they then filled with a mix of water and milk; they put them in the freezer at home and made frozen pigeons. Eventually this solution was cheaper than the clay pigeons they had used to buy. Furthermore, they didn't have to retrieve any pigeons from the field so they didn't damage the crops anymore. And the ban was lifted.

Personal Analogy

1. Starting formulation
2. First round
3. Select a crucial object from the problem context
4. How would you feel if you were this object in this particular situation?
5. How would you react if you felt like this?
6. What would you do?
7. Resociate

TIP FOR THE COACH

PERSONAL ANALOGY REQUIRES A HIGH DEGREE OF EMPATHY AND IMAGINATION. IT IS NOT A SUITABLE TECHNIQUE FOR EVERYONE. HOWEVER, PEOPLE WHO ARE CAPABLE OF APPLYING PERSONAL ANALOGY LIKE IT A LOT AND FIND IT VERY EFFICIENT. THESE PEOPLE USUALLY REPRESENT ONLY A THIRD OF A RANDOM GROUP WHICH MAKES IT A LITTLE MORE DIFFICULT TO APPLY WITHIN IN GROUP SITUATIONS. NEVERTHELESS, PERSONAL ANALOGY IS AN IDEAL TECHNIQUE FOR SOLVING TECHNICAL PROBLEMS AND IS VERY USEFUL IN PRODUCT DEVELOPMENT.

Random Stimulation

What is it? In the former techniques you are the one in control of the course of action. You search for presuppositions, you pick an analogon or a hero, you feel the feelings of a chosen object. With the technique of random stimulation you let go of all of this and allow coincidence to decide what kind of information will help you to solve the problem. It can be exciting!

This technique begins with the conviction that in your mind you can link any two things together. We can assure you – it works if you believe in it! Beginning with any randomly chosen information, your brain will link back to the problem situation with more or less effort.

It might sound like an odd technique. However, random stimulation is very efficient (and exceptionally fast) once you are proficient at basic skills such as resociation, using your imagination and toppling words. For this reason it is sometimes considered as the best technique for experienced creative thinkers or for people with a natural aptitude for creative thinking.

How does the technique work? It is extremely simple. Using random stimulation means that you choose non-problem-related information to inspire you. The choice should always be made at random. You let fate decide.

A. Gathering random information. A convenient method is to choose a word from a magazine or a newspaper you have at hand or may even have bought for this purpose. The word can be chosen using a set pattern. For instance, 'Take the first meaningful word on page 21, second column, third line.' You can then use this word to solve the problem.

It is important that this word is meaningful because you need random information to stimulate your imagination. *This sentence consists of five meaningful words.* (They are: sentence-consists-five-meaningful-words). It is clearly much more difficult to associate with 'this' and 'of'. Random information might also consist of a picture from the magazine, for example an advertisement or a photo. Experience tells us, though, that resociating from images is usually more difficult to accomplish.

B. Once the random information is available, you begin by forming a number of associations around the random concept. Starting from these associations you then resociate towards the starting formulation.

For example: If the random word is 'Taj Mahal' you could make the following associations:

The real challenge consists of resociating from these associations back towards the starting formulation. You don't necessarily have to write down the associations although it is useful, especially when working in a group.

An alternative way of working is to resociate directly from 'Taj Mahal' towards the starting formulation. This process of resociation will then prob-ably use the same pathways as the method explained above. However, this process is faster and you will feel less in control of things.

Random Stimulation

1. Starting formulation
2. First round
3. Choose random information: a word, an image, a photo, an object, a sound...
4. Associate around this random information
5. Resociate

Your turn

Think of an original activity for next weekend, something you can do on your own or with your family. Draw inspiration from *Creativity Today*. Say a random page number out loud. Turn to the page and take the word or the image exactly in the centre of that page. Think of five ideas for this weekend, always postponing judgement.

TIP FOR THE COACH

The following questions arise in some groups:
How long do we have to resociate from a given term? Until you have gathered a certain amount of ideas. Don't get too easily discouraged. The less obviously the random element is related to the problem, the better; then you must really force your brain to make new connections.

Can we use different words one after the other? Of course, but make sure you don't make it too easy for yourself. Don't switch to the next word too fast simply because you don't like the first one.

What is 'bad' random information? The only real bad luck you can have is that the random information is by coincidence completely related to the problem context. This won't generate new information, so just choose another word.

When should we apply this technique? You can apply the random stimulation technique to any kind of problem. It is a very convenient technique to use after trying various other techniques. You can use random stimulation as a 'quick last go' to see if it generates any other surprising ideas, and this often happens.

On the sofa
My friend Paul is an architect and describes himself as a hedonist.
In fact this just means that he was born tired. This affects the way
he applies creative thinking. When he starts a new design job, he
lies down on the sofa, a pint of beer within easy reach. He takes
a magazine, any magazine, which he then leafs through, taking
his time and not tiring himself out, until a new idea 'jumps' into
his mind.

This example offers a variation on the random stimulation technique. You
don't 'choose' the random information but you let all kinds of information
seep into your mind. You could for instance pick up an illustrated book, a
newspaper or a magazine, or you could surf the Internet. When you're driving
on the motorway, you could let billboards or the logos on trucks be your
source of inspiration. Just don't forget to keep the starting formulation in mind.

Next you wait for your mind to make new connections between the
random information and the given issue. All kinds of wild connections can
result from this but be patient and wait until, eureka, a useful connection
arises that helps you with the problem. This particular variation is closely
related to the technique of free incubation.

Free Incubation

What is it? Incubation is similar to taking distance from the logical context
of the problem. The distance can be mental but also physical. 'Incubation'
refers to a period during the creative process in which your attention is not
focused on the problem and in which you let your mind wander. Your brain,
however, will be unconsciously occupied with the problem and lets the information simmer and mature in your subconscious. This may suddenly lead to
a Eureka moment, when the brain offers a solution to a problem that you
were not consciously exploring right then.

During the process of free incubation you should let incubation do its
work without forcing anything. The only thing you deliberately do is to
create distance. Sensibly inserting incubation time into your creative session
can vastly improve the quality of the creative process. It is generally advisable
to take a break from conscious effort from time to time when dealing with
tough problems and to introduce incubation periods, rather than trying to
come up with a solution in one go.

Many famous people have had important breakthroughs which came
about during incubation. Who doesn't remember the story of Archimedes
who experienced his Eureka moment when he stepped into his bath? He
saw the water rise and instantly understood that he could measure the
volume of any given object by immersion in water.

Another example of incubation: in 1865, the scientist August Kékulé von Stradonitz saw the mythical image of the Ourobouros in a dream, the snake or dragon that bites its own tail. This inspired a whole new hypothesis on the shape of the benzene molecule (C6H6).

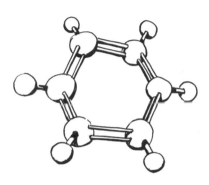

How does the technique work? Free incubation is best applied after a strenuous diverging phase. Some degree of frustration through exhaustion of ideas during the first and the second round can even be helpful. This feeling of dissatisfaction signals to the brain that the problem is important. It stimulates the mind 'not to forget' this problem.

Free incubation is a very easy technique to organise but no one can explain how it actually works. You should try to discover the best way of personally putting a problem 'out of your mind'. One disadvantage of this technique is that you seem to have little impact on the process. Yet every creative thinker will find out sooner or later which incubation strategies work best for him or her.

Free Incubation
1. Starting formulation
2. First round
3. Possible second round
4. Lay the problem aside. Take distance (mental, physical)
5. Wait and see

Incubation Methods

Taking distance can be done in various ways. You can mentally work on **another assignment** (for instance solve another problem) or do some housework (wash up, chop wood, mow the lawn…).

Relaxation proves to be a very successful incubation method for many people: taking a bath or a shower, sauna, lying on your back in the sun, daydreaming, losing yourself in easy listening, classical or lounge music… The brain switches to another rhythm than its usual daytime one.

Eastern meditation and relaxation techniques can help you to reach the same 'remote' attitude that free incubation aims at. Yoga, Tai Chi, Zen meditation fit into this list.

Physical exercise can stimulate mental relaxation. Walking, running, cycling, rollerblading and skating are sports which also provide physical distance from the problem context. 'Sleeping on it' and making love are of course tried and tested incubation methods as well.

Others prefer to move to a **new environment** that stimulates them to think differently. You can leave your desk and go to another room, sit in the garden or go out and lose yourself in the crowd at a train station or in a pub.

Movement (in the sense of 'locomotion') appears to be very inspiring for many people: driving on a motorway, a train journey, an airplane flight...

The bottom line is that you should find your own mix of incubation methods that you feel comfortable with and that work well for you. You will know what works for you after you have done it for a while.

PLAGIARISM IS COPYING FROM ONE SOURCE
RESEARCH IS COPYING FROM TWO OR MORE
anonymous

TIP FOR THE COACH

If you want to introduce incubation during a creative session you can also choose to stage a playful intermediate brainstorm. This means seeking solutions to a playful problem.

It not only allows you to create distance but also offers the opportunity to practise creative thinking in the group and to train the rules of diverging. A playful brainstorm is a rewarding warm-up exercise that usually doesn't take more than five minutes. It can create a positive atmosphere that you should try to maintain during the entire creative session.

Of course you can also suggest a break in the creative session in order to stimulate free incubation. You can temporarily stop the session for a long walk or even let several nights pass. If so, don't forget to tell the participants to bring their new ideas to the following meeting.

It is useful to tell the participants to always have a notebook and pen at hand so that they can write down any thoughts or brainwaves. This ensures that no ideas are lost during incubation. Experience tells us that ideas that spontaneously arise, also spontaneously disappear in a short time and are easily lost.

Guided Imagery

What is it? Using guided imagery you make use of a script to guide incubation instead of letting it run freely. The scenario creates distance to the problem; it also provides elements of inspiration and appropriate moments for resociation.

'Imagery' is processing information by means of mental images that come from the deeper layers of our thought system. (See also page 33, developing imagination). This ability is active and useful countless times during our daily life, mostly unconsciously. Using guided imagery, we will consciously make use of these images.

Not everybody feels comfortable with imagation techniques such as guided imagery. You have to be able to lose yourself in the process and trust that your brain is able to do more than you can control. Take your time and trust in yourself.

There are different ways to start using guided imagery. You can make a habit of exercising your mind with fantasy games, like Einstein did. You can also structure the process more and write scripts for yourself or others that will allow the incubation process to generate new insights. You use these scripts to give the subconscious a number of 'assignments' and see what kinds of solutions are generated.

Guided imagery can be applied in areas like vision and product development. For example, one group at the Aalsmeer Flower Auction (the biggest in the world) used guided imagery to come up with concepts for future flower shops. However, guided imagery also works for concrete and short-term problems.

In *Creativity Today* we won't venture too deeply into this type of creativity method. However, it is useful for you to know that this exists and might work for you. If you want to learn more, please look at the bibliography for suitable books on the subject.

How does the technique work? Before starting the session you will have thought up a short imagery script for yourself, another person or for a group of people, and a number of assignments. The script should be concrete enough to guide the thought process into the desired directions, but first of all leave enough space for the imaginative power of the practitioner.

Guided imagery works best in a peaceful, quiet environment. Choose a silent room, relax, breathe evenly and close your eyes. Dedicate enough time to preparation when coaching another person or a group with this guided imagery technique. Next the scenario is rolled out. You should open yourself up to the images that arise in your mind and observe what happens. When the guided imagery trip is finished, the images and symbols collected are applied to the problem context. You should try to translate them into concrete solutions to the problem.

Where do you get your best ideas?
I don't, they get me Alan Fletcher

Guided Imagery
0. A scenario has been thought up beforehand
1. Starting formulation
2. First ideas
3. Relax
4. Begin with the scenario
5. Open up to mental images
6. After the guided imagery: resociate from the images and symbols

Example
Here is one example of a guided imagery exercise. You can apply this exercise yourself to a subject of your choice. Tip: take a look at what you have written on the coasters on page 55.

First focus on your question for a while...

We will now tell you a story in which you play the leading role. Try to experience the story to the full and make an effort to imagine the sensory perceptions of everything you encounter...

You're walking on a beautiful exotic beach. You feel the sand beneath your feet and in between your toes. Your hair is blowing in the wind. You walk along the shore for a while...
   In the distance you see a village. There is a party going on. You can hear the music when you draw closer. People are dancing. It's a wonderful party. Everyone is happy. You mingle in the crowd...
   After a while, a small building a little further away catches your attention. You know that someone will be waiting for you there, someone with the best intentions towards you and who knows what you are searching for. You know that this person will welcome you with presents. You walk slowly towards the building and enter...
   The person is happy to see you and welcomes you...
The person leads you into another room and gives you the presents. You accept them. You thank the person and have a good look at the presents...
   After a while you say goodbye, pick up the presents and walk back along the beach...

You now return to this room...

You open your eyes...

Now imagine how the information from the guided imagery tour can be helpful in answering the question you started with.

TIP FOR THE COACH

PLEASE BE CAREFUL WHEN YOU PERFORM A GUIDED IMAGERY EXERCISE WITH ANOTHER PERSON OR A GROUP. BE WELL PREPARED AND TEST THE SCENARIO BEFOREHAND. FOR INSTANCE, IT IS VERY IMPORTANT TO SET THE STORY IN THE RIGHT FRAMEWORK. AS ALWAYS WITH ANY TECHNIQUE PRACTICE MAKES PERFECT.

OF COURSE NOT EVERYONE IS READY OR SUITABLE FOR THIS KIND OF CREATIVE TECHNIQUE. EVEN SO, WE SEE THAT MANY PEOPLE WITH EXPERIENCE OF THE MORE COGNITIVE TECHNIQUES WILL BE OPEN TO GUIDED IMAGERY.

When to Use Which Technique?

The diverging techniques we have described differ in several ways. Each technique has its strong points, each its own line of approach. We want to stress that you can apply different methods one after the other. The most important thing when choosing a method is your own preference. You will probably notice that the techniques you like most will generate the best results. These will also be the techniques that you are best at when working with groups.

How do you know what suits you best? Trial and error. However, there are certain general differences that should be mentioned. You will find some practical tips on the next page. These apply to yourself and to the group profile when working collectively.

	Incubation time	Threshold	Range	Specific Demands	When to Apply
Presuppositions	fast	low	broad	ability to question your own thinking	not with personal or emotional topics
Direct Analogy	fast	low	broad	a minimum of playfulness	always applicable
Superhero	fast	low	broad	a minimum of playfulness	always applicable
Personal Analogy	fast	high	deep	strong empathy	best for technical topics
Random Stimulation	very fast	medium	wide	experience with resociation	best in combination with other techniques
Free Incubation	slow	low	deep	sufficient time	if you have enough time
Guided Imagery	medium	high	deep	openness	best not used with inexperienced groups

TIP FOR THE COACH

The golden rule is that you are at your best when you enjoy what you are doing! Here is some advice for the creativity coach who wants to become proficient in group work.

Incubation Time The different techniques each have their own way of dealing with incubation time. Free incubation is unconstrained and as such is a relatively 'slow' technique because you 'wait' until a solution emerges. The other techniques also include one form of incubation or another but they deliberately take a shortcut by applying a structured way of creating distance and resociating.

Guided imagery is an intermediate form involving the deeper layers of thought during the search for solutions. The five other techniques are rather fast techniques which mean that the incubation will not reach the same depth. They focus on making new connections rapidly. The most rational of the five techniques is using presuppositions.

Low Versus High Threshold Techniques Our experience with hundreds of creative sessions has taught us that personal analogy and guided imagery create on average the greatest barrier. Yet, they are extremely efficient for creative thinkers gifted with plenty of empathy and a large emotive imagination. Direct analogy on the other hand is accessible to a large number of people and is very suitable for large groups.

Applicability The presupposition technique is widely applicable and particularly advisable for technical and organisational assignments. It is not advised to apply this technique to personal or psychological problems. Direct analogy and superhero are widely applicable to a wide range of assignments and groups. Personal analogy is ideal for topics with a strong technical aspect and when the participants are open to it. Time and commitment are the key factors in the application of free incubation. Successful guided imagery with a group requires an experienced coach.

Quality Versus Quantity or Depth Versus Breadth Quality does not mean better ideas but more elaborate ideas. Either you choose a technique that aims at generating a large number of ideas in a short time – the quality should then result from the quantity; or you choose a technique that will generate a limited number of better-developed and more elaborate ideas.

The presupposition technique rapidly leads to new breakthrough ideas and works in stages. Direct analogy is certainly the easiest diverging technique. Superhero and random stimulation are broad techniques and will generate fewer ideas with inexperienced groups. Personal analogy, free incubation and guided imagery go less for quantity and more for profundity. They generate more sensitive ideas with more emotional involvement.

Alongside the techniques described above, a large number of alternative methods can be found in literature and on the Internet. You will gradually develop your own working methods. The German playwright, Schiller, for instance, used to write best with the smell of rotting apples in his room. Author Emile Zola preferred to work in artificial light. While writing *Creativity Today*, the authors made several train journeys between the Belgian city of Ghent and the coast because train travel inspires them.

In order to put all of this new knowledge into practice, we now invite you to move on to the training section. A range of interesting topics will serve as practise and training material for creative diverging.

Almost all really new ideas have a certain aspect of foolishness when they are first produced
Alfred N. Whitehead

DIVERGING PHASE

Resociation

Why? Resociation is a conscious thought activity. During the diverging phase you connect to the problem context in a controlled way, starting from an element or a topic that is at first sight not related to the problem. Some of these new connections will provide new insights into the subject, and may even offer new solutions. Resociation is part of all creativity techniques.

How? You resociate by directing your attention. You can find out how this works by doing the exercises below.

Exercises !

An imagination exercise: Picture yourself driving a vehicle down the motorway on your way to a certain destination. You have plenty of time and you find this particular road rather boring, you would like to see something else. You decide to take a side-road as a detour and so you leave the motorway. You're on a journey of discovery, you follow country lanes and you let the environment surprise you.

After a relaxed drive around for a while you decide to head for your final destination again. You know the goal, you instinctively feel where the main road is and you trust that you remember the right direction. You 'forge a new path' and find another route to your target. This is an evocative way of describing resociation.

Read the following association exercise and think up images for it.
Tour de France – yellow jersey – sun – Spain – bull fight – torero

Now make some associative chains between 'torero' and 'Tour de France' using a maximum of three links. Two examples:

torero – hero – Lance Armstrong – Tour de France
torero – arena – circus – caravan – Tour de France

Now find another five.

Exercises !!!

You are searching for ideas for a pleasant weekend trip with friends or colleagues. Jot down around five ideas. These first ideas will give an indication of your frame of thought; they are the first patterns.

STOP searching,
START creating

Ramon Vullings

Let the following words inspire you. For each word think of three new ideas for your weekend trip.

- Picasso
- Benedictine monastery
- a watch
- Mars

On page 232 you will find some sample answers.

The following exercises on diverging techniques will automatically offer further training in resociation.

Presuppositions

Why? Conscious and unconscious presuppositions keep new ideas out of reach. That's why we need to find these presuppositions and challenge them in order to allow for new ideas to develop.

How?
First Method

1. Starting formulation
2. First round
3. Select crucial terms in the starting formulation
4. Determine the presupposition for every term used
5. Ask yourself for every presupposition: What if I eliminated or reversed it?
6. Resociation (new ideas)

Second Method

1. Starting formulation
2. First round
3. Write down the common characteristics of the first ideas.
   These indicate presuppositions
4. Ask yourself for every presupposition: What if I eliminated or reversed it?
5. Resociation (new ideas)

Exercises !

Write down some presuppositions concealed within the following concepts:

- second-hand cars
- sunglasses
- success
- immigrants
- pupils
- development aid

Have a look at page 233 for a few examples regarding second-hand cars.

Exercises !!!

Pick a sensitive subject from your own personal or work context, something that is at the forefront of your mind at the moment. If you like, you can go back to page 55 and add this subject to your list.

Compose your own starting formulation. Take one or two crucial concepts from it and list eight presuppositions for each. The first ones will be the conscious presuppositions. Try to go beyond these. Now have a talk with a family member or colleague and ask for their help in finding five more interesting presuppositions, things you hadn't thought of at first.

Imagine (or perhaps you don't need to) that you are tired of your current occupation. Here is a way of finding out what kind of other work might suit you. Apply the second presupposition method to this exercise.

- Write down a number of jobs you would like to do
- Consider their common features
- Now reverse each presupposition and diverge around possible activities, always postponing judgement.

If you want to make a selection of ideas now, we would advise using the COCD box (see Chapter Six, page 135).

Sometimes the habits and convictions of people who lived in former times can surprise us. Centuries ago almost everybody was convinced that the sun turned around the earth. In the medical field, bloodletting was a generally accepted treatment. These beliefs persisted for quite some time.

It is certain that at the beginning of the 21st century we keep alive a large number of presuppositions that will surprise our descendants. An interesting group exercise is to search for presuppositions in our current society.

Adopt the viewpoint of someone looking back a hundred years from now at the beginning of the 21st century, someone surprised by the behaviour and convictions of today's world. What common presuppositions do we have?

Direct Analogy

Why? You can bypass your mental thought patterns by forging new connections. An 'analogon' that has nothing to do with your subject matter can provide assistance.

INNOVATION IS EVERYTHING YO

How?

1. Starting formulation
2. First round
3. Choose an analogon
4. What is specific about this analogon?
   Write down its characteristics and the associations you have with it
5. Make every feature a starting point in the search for new ideas.
   Resociate

Exercises !

Devise an 'association flower' using the following words (see page 98, example Taj Mahal):

- red deer
- saw
- spacecraft
- apartment

Choose an analogon: list ten subjects you are interested in and which inspire you. Choose one of them and draw an association flower, as above, with at least 25 different associations. Repeat this with another topic from the list of ten.

Exercises !!!

A young teenager you're acquainted with has a problem. He/she would like to earn some money but is too young for an official holiday job. Think up a number of ways for this teenager to earn some money during the next school holiday. Use the direct analogy technique to tackle this.

Every summer the Red Cross has to deal with a shortage of blood during the summer season. The main cause is that its regular blood donors are on holiday. The Red Cross would like to be better prepared the following summer. It plans to start a major campaign in the spring to attract new donors.

You are asked to come up with ideas to attract new donors in your region. Think up ideas by means of the direct analogy technique.

Superhero

Why? Heroes stimulate our imagination. They are able to achieve more than we can. Why don't we 'ask them to solve the problem'? They have so much more freedom than we (think we) have.

How?

1. Starting formulation
2. First round
3. Choose a hero or a heroine
4. Bring your hero or your heroine to life
   Which qualities can you give him or her?
5. How would your hero or heroine tackle the problem?
6. Translate the suggestions into concrete solutions for the problem.
   Resociate

Exercises !

Think back to your youth. Who were your heroes at the time? Can you remember why they were so special?

List ten heroes: half of them should be (living or deceased) people and half of them fantasy figures.

Exercises !!!

One of your friends has a child who needs a little stimulation to help around the house. You are asked to come up with some incentives.

Think of an actual child you know. Try to think of some original rewards that won't cost you (or the parents) any money and that will be a real incentive for the teenager to fulfil the tasks with pleasure.

In some regions the law courts are experiencing a delay in the treatment of cases. Think of new ways to reduce the delay to an acceptable minimum over a period of two years without undermining security.

Personal Analogy

Why? This technique offers a completely different way of considering technical problems. Using your empathy, you imagine that you are an object. You abandon rational thought and automatically find yourself looking at the problem from a totally different angle.

How?

1. Starting formulation
2. First round
3. Select a crucial object from the problem context
4. How would you feel if you were this object in that particular situation?
5. How would you react if you felt this way? What kind of thing would you do?
6. Resociate

Exercises !

How would you feel if you were the book *Creativity Today* that you're holding in your hands? What would you (being *Creativity Today*) change about yourself in order to become even more attractive to the reader? What would you want to tell the reader?

Imagine that you are your own car, or if you don't have a car, your bicycle. What are you like as a vehicle? Are you satisfied with yourself? What are your strong and weak points? What is your character like? What kind of trips do you like best? How do you feel when you're out and you meet other vehicles?

Exercises !!!

Children don't like brushing their teeth every day and often forget to do it. Apply the personal analogy technique to try and find new ways of motivating children on a permanent basis to brush their teeth. Imagine these real children, children you know, in a bathroom that you know.

As an analogon, you can choose all kinds of things from the environment of the 'toothbrusher'. You can be the toothbrush, breakfast, the bathroom mirror, etc. (also see the training section on page 119).

Meetings often don't run smoothly and could be a lot shorter. The traditional meeting techniques (start on time, use and respect the agenda, etc.) are not always sufficient or don't always work in practice. Why don't you try to find an original solution for a specific meeting problem? An advertising agency in Norway, for example, has a meeting room with a high table and no chairs. This is the room where decisions are made.

Imagine a specific meeting you regularly attend. Think about what goes wrong, about a problem that regularly occurs. First think of solutions and then use the technique of personal analogy to find more original ways of enhancing that specific meeting.

Random Stimulation

Why? You are surrounded by all kinds of information that can inspire you to deal with your problems and create new opportunities. When you have become proficient at resociating you will collect new ideas just by looking around you.

How?
1. Starting formulation
2. First round
3. Choose random information: a word, an image or a photograph, an object, a sound...
4. Associate around the random information
5. Resociate

Exercises !

You will soon have a weekend to yourself. Use random stimulation to think of a series of activities you could do. Only decide afterwards what you're really going to do.

A young boy or girl has been grounded but wants to go outside and play. Think of original ways of leaving the bedroom while the parents still think that the child has stayed there all day. Use the random stimulation technique.

Exercises !!!

A friend has just graduated as a fashion designer. She would like to show her new collection in an unusual way. Think of an original location and an original concept for this fashion show, within the budgetary limitations of a student.

Apply a variation of the random stimulation technique when you are confronted with a problem or a question today or tomorrow. At that moment, look in your diary or address book. Pick an arbitrary telephone number and call that person. Tell him or her that this is a creativity exercise and propose thinking of new ideas together.

'If everythings seems under control, you're not going fast enough.' Mario Andretti

Here is a totally different assignment! Consider synchronicity as a concept. What if coincidence isn't just random... Note the coincidental circumstances that happen to you over the following week and ask yourself if these could harbour a specific meaning for you.

Free Incubation

Why? Your brain continues to process a problem even when your attention is no longer focusing on it. You can deliberately use this process while looking for new solutions. You give your mind 'an assignment' while you do something else.

How?

1. Starting formulation
2. First round
3. If necessary, second round
4. Put the problem aside. Step back mentally and/or physically (see page 101)
5. Wait and see

Exercise !

Try to find out which methods of free incubation already work for you.

Exercises !!!

Free incubation only works if you are dealing with a subject that really matters to you. For that reason choose a subject from page 55 or another problem that you would really like to solve. Try out some of the methods on page 101. You will only believe in free incubation once it really works but you won't find this out without an open mind.

Over the next six months read a book or go on a course that treats the non-rational aspects of thought.

Guided Imagery

Why? The guided imagery technique is based on trusting your own wisdom and imaginative power. It enables you to open up to information in the deeper layers of your mind. A scenario helps to give this a framework.

How?

0. Write a scenario beforehand
1. Starting formulation
2. First ideas
3. Time to relax
4. Begin the scenario
5. Be open to the inner images generated by the script
6. After the guided imagery: resociate from the images and the symbols

Exercises !

All exercises on imaginative power in Chapter Two on page 44 are good starting exercises as preparation for this technique.

Apply the guided imagery exercise on page 105 to a number of different subjects.

Exercises !!!

Your local city centre police invite you to a brainstorming session. They are experiencing problems with theft on the subway and in buses because of the activities of a professional network of pickpockets. The traditional prevention and control methods have already been employed to no avail. Think of some original ways of catching the pickpockets red-handed. Complete this exercise using guided imagery.

Guided imagery is a technique you can develop. If you want to become really proficient, we recommend that you read specific literature on the subject and gain more experience. The bibliography lists a number of helpful books on the subject.

TODAY   CATEGORY Designer case study

SUBJECT Tables

ASSIGNMENT Diverge on the theme 'tables'

BRIEFING

You can also apply the preceding techniques to the designer case studies on pages 74 to 76. You will find some brief advice below. In the next chapter you can also read about the results of others' attempts at these problems. Remember though – you will learn more by thinking up new ideas yourself.

Don't forget to always start the diverging phase with a first round of spontaneous ideas generated without applying any technique.

Design original tables

For the diverging phase regarding this assignment we would advise that you work with the following techniques in turn:
- presuppositions (second method)
- direct analogy
- guided imagery

Folding Table

Anti-Spill Table

'Tea-for-Two'

TODAY   CATEGORY Designer case study

SUBJECT Toothbrushes

ASSIGNMENT Diverge on the theme 'toothbrushes'

Think of some original toothbrushes
The application of the following techniques will generate surprising new ideas for this subject:
- personal analogy
- random stimulation
- free incubation

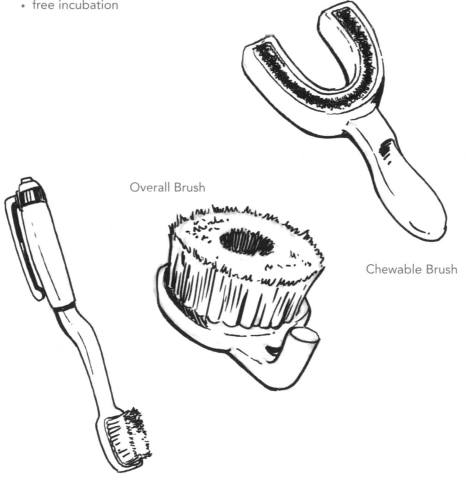

Overall Brush

Chewable Brush

Breast Pocket Brush

TODAY   CATEGORY Designer case study

SUBJECT Bridges

ASSIGNMENT Diverge on the theme 'bridges'

Imagine bridge concepts
The following techniques are very suitable for this technical assignment:
- presuppositions
- the super hero
- free incubation

Castle Bridge

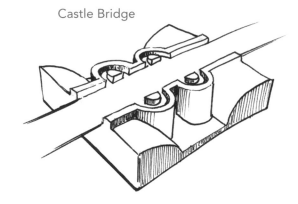

Airlift Bridge

TODAY   CATEGORY Organisation case study

SUBJECT Railway strike

DESCRIPTION Starting formulation

The briefing can be found on page 77. Here you will find a number of possibilities for starting formulations as well as a list of ideas from the divergent phase generated by a creative group. The group used the direct analogy technique, after a long first round of ideas. Naturally, judgement was postponed.

Possible starting statements for the case study:
1. Think of some things you could do which might cause the management to call a halt to the planned reorganisation and at the same time offer a salary increase. These activities must be undertaken in such a way as to win the sympathy of railway passengers and the general public.

2. Think of alternatives to a railway strike which might influence the company and still win the sympathy of the train passengers.

3. How can we persuade management to adjust the planned organisational changes to include our wishes, without negatively affecting customer service?

4. How can we strongly insure that management takes our wishes into account, while we still gain the public's sympathy?

5. How can we insure that management takes into account the wishes of the trade union and at the same time doesn't lose the public's sympathy or diminish customer service levels?

6. How can we insure that the reorganisation doesn't take place?

7. How do we get a pay raise?

8. How do we win the sympathy of the public?

9. How can we convince management to stop the proposed reorganisation, offer a pay raise and for us to win the sympathy of railway clients and the public?

Number 4 was chosen.

How can we strongly insure that management takes our wishes into account, while we still gain the public's sympathy?

Ideas from the First Round
1. Discuss matters with the management team
2. Think of alternative plans
3. Work out the financial impact of a salary increase and arguments for it
4. Ask management to hire temporary workers
5. Talk to the public in train stations and explain the problems
6. 'Work-to-rule' at railway stations which wouldn't affect passengers in a negative way
7. Organise a strike in the administration department with no negative impact on the public
8. Incite strikes in other organisations (postal or transport) to give the railway a good image in contrast (we are working!)
9. Work without pay. Conductors give up their pay (Gandhi approach) or give their pay to a good cause
10. Trains run and passengers do not pay (payment strike)
11. Reduce prices for passengers
12. Work with a decrease in pay while taking action
13. Write a book with background information about the situation and the problems
14. Offer the public the opportunity to work as a train conductor for a day (with the assistance of a pro)
15. Create an Internet site to inform the public of the problems
16. Create an Internet site to collect creative ideas
17. Make contact with colleagues abroad
18. Have train conductors set themselves on fire to get attention
19. Let youth groups work on the trains for free tickets
20. Extra services on the trains to gain press coverage
21. Everyone can travel 1st class for the price of 2nd class
22. Trains to run on time for a whole day
23. Put web-cams in the drivers' compartments so that passengers get to know the job better
24. Write an article about the working week of a conductor
25. Paint the trains in bright colours to get attention
26. Paint trains in dark colours to get attention
27. Let graffiti artists go wild on the trains
28. Write poetry on the outside of the trains
29. Write slogans on the trains

30. Hand out pamphlets
31. Work with the management step by step – agreements could be made over time
32. Television advertising – to challenge certain issues
33. Create and market a train simulation game for children
34. Create and market a rail company management game
35. Conductors can give courses at model train clubs to give people more insight into the job
36. Extra comforts for conductors (e.g. a lounge area)
37. Improve train technology (better seats and security systems)
38. Improve technology in the trains (LCD screen, computer connection…) for passengers' use and ask other unions if they can install the products for a lower price (as volunteer work)
39. Send text messages with arrival and departure times
40. Improve safety at railway stations with 'neighbourhood watch' for train conductors
41. Reconsider the configuration of seating and tables in the trains
42. Offer a place for conductors to sleep in the locomotive
43. An idea box for conductors
44. Invite management out for lunch or dinner
45. Pick up management by taxi from their homes and take them to work by train
46. Ask members of the management to be a conductor once a week (i.e. McDonald's method)
47. 'Train Conductor Aid' project – help for the poor
48. Free train tickets
49. Have a carnival in a station
50. Have a dressing-up party for conductors and ticket inspectors
51. Party train
52. Paint all our demands/wishes on the train
53. Hand out two leaflets, one which lists the conductors' wishes and one which lists the wishes of the management. Organise a vote by the public the following week in a train station
54. 'Big Brother' in the train
55. Apply restructuring activities virtually. (For example: Station X would be closed, hang banners in station X with the text 'If the management implements the restructuring, this train will not stop here anymore')
56. Wreck one of the management team's cars and make a TV report
57. Let everyone travel on the train for a symbolic fee (e.g. one dollar, one euro, one pound)
58. Bonus payments for staff who arrive to work on time
59. Hire more people

60. Encourage the public to take the train
61. Improve comfort within the trains
62. Choose the best idea of the year from the 'idea box'
63. Fun activities
64. Promote job sharing
65. Spray the trains in bright colours (e.g. red) to show how unhappy we are
66. Draw up a petition
67. Have free public transport days
68. Ask the Minister of Transport to become a conductor for a day
69. Plan entertainment events in the train
70. Create 'theme trains'
71. Create 'Travel Museums'
72. Add restaurants to the trains
73. Hold fashion shows on the train
74. Let men and women work on alternate days
75. Let the public graffiti the train wagons
76. Contract work with taxi companies to insure that passengers get to where they want to go
77. Clients will be helped to get to where they want to go by other means of transport (taxi, buses, tram, and metro)
78. Play a song in the trains that helps people to understand our wishes
79. A railway pub crawl: at every stop you have a drink in the café
80. Train-tram-bike day. Every person who gets on the train with his/her bike gets a free breakfast
81. 'Travel With Your Pet Day'
82. Get the public to take the train for a day and everyone travels free and gets a free breakfast
83. A 'Guinness World Record Day' where the longest train in the world will be made
84. Let the train stop for one minute at every crossing
85. 'Guinness Book of Records' how many people can fit in one wagon?
86. Have 'school in the train' with striking teachers
87. E-mail bombardment of the top ten railway managers
88. Change National Train Day into a National Bus Day
89. Competition: How do you survive on a conductor's salary?
90. Night Week: Trains run throughout the night
91. Study day at a university to focus on the problem we are having
92. A questionnaire to collect creative ideas
93. One week to travel experiencing the wishes of the personnel and another week to travel according to management wishes
94. Hire train clowns
95. Build a model railway at company HQ

96. Have all trains depart 5 minutes early
97. Free train travel for widows, mentally/physically disabled…
98. Free trains to all eastern European countries for rejected asylum seekers
99. Make conductors' schedules more flexible
100. Install metal detectors
101. 'Buy Two and Get One Free' Day
102. Develop unexpected electrical failure and ask the passengers to pull the train
103. Reorganisation simulation – let all the trains run with half the personnel
104. Everybody to work 16 instead of 8 hour shifts and then get 32 hours off
105. Combine two trains' worth of passengers and have every second train on the timetable run
106. FTM programmes (Frequent Train Miles programme like they have on airplanes)
107. Create an event where passengers get on a train but don't know where it will stop
108. Night-time orientation hikes (passengers dropped off by train)
109. Announced strikes
110. No ticket control
111. Medals for the passengers who are hardest hit by the changes
112. Pancakes on the train
113. Give out free traveller's cheques up to 25 euros
114. A charity soccer game
115. Children's Day on the trains: take a look behind the scenes
116. Passengers take over work of the personnel
117. Explain how to use the emergency brake
118. Hire clowns with balloons
119. A 'Save the Conductor' Day
120. Cook waffles on the train
121. Train ride where the whistle blows constantly
122. Party train with a huge disco
123. Erotic train exhibition
124. Go crazy on the train for 24 hours
125. A night strike
126. Free parking for passengers
127. Free catering on Intercity trains
128. One free ticket with every ticket sold
129. Extra supplement in the Metro newspaper
130. Technical personnel will give the stations an extra cleaning
131. Close all the level crossings for a period of time
132. All students get a weekend pass
133. All students receive a 'my train was late' pass

134. Free 'après train' bar at all station exits
135. All women receive a rose
136. Free 'strike lotto' in partnership with the national lottery
137. All trains to arrive very, very late
138. No heating in the trains in the winter
139. Randomly choose not to stop at some stations
140. Costume party for all passengers
141. Naked service
142. Theme wagons
143. Create a new announcement system
144. Exchange the whistle for an animal noise
145. Special tickets with extra information (A4 sized)
146. Special T-shirts for personnel
147. Don't clean the trains for a few weeks
148. Organise a theatre performance at the station
149. Personnel can bring their children to work
150. Lay out a red carpet in the train
151. Hand out a free magazine or newspaper
152. Paint the tracks a different colour
153. Flashing lights in the carriages
154. Meeting rooms at the station
155. Ironing for passengers in the train station

Second Round of Ideas, Using the Direct Analogy Technique

Direct Analogy with an Ape as Analogue
156. Take off shoes before boarding the train (**four hands**)
157. Decorating overhead wires (**climbing**)
158. Free electricity offered via overhead wires
159. Build a climbing wall on the outside of HQ
160. Create your own hourly schedule (**imitating**)
161. Wear a label that says 'Today I Am Also a Passenger'
162. Throw eggs at the management (**throwing**)
163. Swing through the wagons like an ape
164. Throw tickets around the station
165. Dial-a-train ride, we come and pick you up (**flexible**)
166. Rickshaws at the train station
167. Campfire on the rails (**tree**)
168. Put banana peel on the stairs in the management building (**banana**)
169. Paint the management's cars yellow
170. Let fleas, mice and snakes loose in the management building (**fleas**)
171. Ultra clean trains

172. Put a train wagon in one of the management team's back gardens
173. Create a petting zoo in the station (**zoo**)
174. Send train conductors' children to the management with a list
     of requests (**kids**)
175. Rugby game against the management
176. A standard timetable delay of exactly five minutes
177. Change trains to 'fire trains'
178. Concert on the train
179. Make a giant nutcracker and crack the management (**nuts**)

Analogy with Cat
180. A 'Happy Rails' idea: a frequent user programme where people can collect
     points (e.g. to visit a vet) (**vet**)
181. Add laser shooting and virtual reality zones to the trains (**friend**)
182. Offer grocery service (**cat food**)
183. Offer services (hairdresser, beauty salon…) on the train (**ginger fur**)
184. Soft toys on the train (**furred**)
185. Offer warm meals and hot drinks (**warmth**)
186. Tracks on top of each other (double capacity) (**speed**)
187. Graffiti advertisements on the wagons (**multicoloured**)
188. Day nurseries on the train (**kitten**)
189. Theme trains (**types of cats**)
190. Radio advertisements on the train (**sharp hearing**)
191. Switch day and night timetables (**nocturnal animal**)
192. Passengers do everything themselves (**independent**)
193. Noah's train: each wagon has a different animal on it (to watch, feel,
     understand) (**farm**)
194. 'Murder on the Orient Express': make the train into a travelling library
     (books and comic books) (**surreptitious**)
195. Funny hijack (**cat and mouse game**)
196. Ancient civilisation trains (**Egyptian God**)
197. Trains powered by solar energy (**independent**)

This group was 'rolling'. They thought of 155 ideas in the first round alone. Using the direct analogy technique the group came up with nearly 200 ideas. From this list, the group selected the best ideas. You will learn how to select ideas in the following chapter on the converging phase.

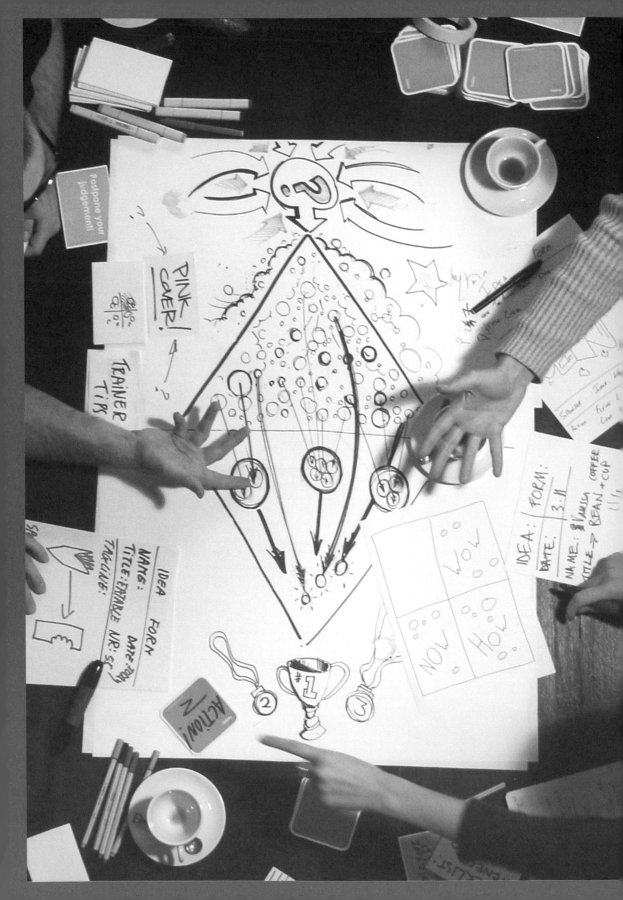

CHAPTER SIX
THE CONVERGING PHASE

In the previous chapter you experienced the pleasure, possibly even the excitement, of diverging. Setting yourself free from fixed thought patterns gives you a liberating feeling. Anything seems possible, everything can be done in a different way! Consequently, it is not surprising that many people identify creativity with this phase. People incorrectly presume that the creative energy can be put away after the diverging phase and that all you need to do now is put the ideas into practice.

Wrong! You are only halfway through the creative process. Of course the diverging phase generates innovative ideas but this is only part of the story. The converging work starts now. You will select, develop, refine, check, correct, and execute. This will require all your creative focus, perhaps even more than the previous stages.

Furthermore, diverging can have a number of disadvantages, especially for groups. The freedom of thought can lead to a loss of focus on your target. As you let go of reality, you might forget that the ideas have to be achieved at some point. Some ideas look terrific but they remain very vague. You can mistake ideas for reality because you see them so clearly that you seriously underestimate the efforts needed to realise these ideas. Or you can enjoy the diverging phase so much that you don't feel like returning to earth. Flying high is much more fun. These are several of the reasons people remain stuck in the diverging phase.

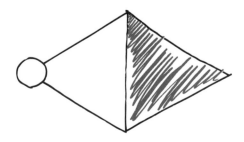

Danger! If you stop the process after diverging, nothing will change. In fact, the ideas don't even really exist yet. They are nothing more than 'new software' in the brain of the conceiver. Quite quickly you will realise that generating ideas is the easiest part of the process. Next comes another kind of creativity, something we call 'converging' creativity and without which nothing new would ever be created.

What is converging all about? Converging is about recognising which ideas have the most potential, developing them into promising concepts, imagining how they will be executed, being able to transmit this image to other people and doing the necessary things to accomplish them. This part of the process uses a different type of creativity. Converging skills include focusing, making intuitive choices, building up concepts, 'syntegrating', activating...

Choosing, Developing, Activating

This theoretical part explains the different steps of the converging phase. This phase is divided into 3 stages: choosing, developing and activating. From an abundance of ideas you will need to choose the ideas with the most potential. You will develop these ideas, strengthen them and build up concepts. Finally you will devise ways to put these new concepts into practice.

For each of these activities we'll provide you with some helpful tools to ensure the converging phase is a success, whether you are on your own or in a group. Try out the techniques that appeal to you. Skip those that don't apply to your particular problem. You can choose from a variety of methods ranging from the fast and simple to extensive converging techniques that you will probably only apply to complicated development processes.

In the training part you will find converging skills that will help you in your personal development. Those who find divergence easy are likely to have more difficulty converging. The training material will guide you through the different skills used, for example, focusing, dealing with abundance, letting go, syntegrating, being decisive, innovating and using your intuition. See what you can learn and apply it!

CHOOSING

The diverging phase will have left you with a multitude of ideas. The number can vary from a few for a tough problem to several hundreds if you have organised a creative session with a group: for instance, to tackle the strike case. Of course you are not able to put all the ideas into practice. In fact you want to dedicate most of your attention to the ideas with potential and very little to those with only minor possibilities. You need to select which to develop and which to leave behind. **The most important question is, of course, what to choose and how?**

IF WE DON'T GET LOST, WE'LL NEVER FIND A NEW ROUTE *Joan Littlewood*

A NEW ROUTE *Joan Littlewood*

Focusing Comes First

Before you start choosing you should refocus on your target and ask yourself if the initial question is still relevant, considering the insights now gained? Are you still as motivated? Are your criteria the same as when you started the creative process? Sure? Then we can start the real process of choosing.

Rationality and Feeling

Choosing has its rational as well as its emotional aspects. Both are important. In your private life as well as in a work context, your rational mind will come up with limitations such as time and money, difficulty of implementation, and so on. Feeling, however, stays in touch with the less tangible aspects that could be important for really innovative cases. Do I like it, does it give me energy, will the customer like this?

It is important to be aware that the more radically innovative the ideas are, the more emotions will play a decisive part in your choice. The reason for this is simple: when we are dealing with radical innovation, there are few or no objective facts available for our minds to work with.

> **Examples**
> Before the introduction of cash dispensers, there was no one single study which suggested that people might want to tap money from the wall if this was technically possible. On the contrary, market research confirmed that customers would always prefer 'a person behind the counter'.
>
> Who would have dared to predict the success of text messaging amongst youngsters? Or that the TV programme *Big Brother*, in all its variations, would become such a huge success all over the world?

Consider the ideas as a kind of raw material from which you will construct the solutions. Your choices should be based on the added value that the ideas will bring to the achievement of your goal. **Beware of the 'creadox' trap!** Feasibility is not the most important criterion in this phase, the added value that an idea or a collection of ideas can offer is.

The Creadox!
A surprising phenomenon takes place when the problem owner is suddenly confronted with a wide variety of ideas after the diverging phase. He will be tempted to play the safe card and to choose the ideas that seem feasible. What he actually does, is choose the ideas that fit within his thought patterns!

The creadox (paradox of creativity) goes like this:
You want something new. You come up with new ideas, but you select the most familiar!

Due to this creadox, creative groups and problem owners are often disillusioned. The mistake they make is to think the only criterion is feasibility, and this blocks the way to real innovation. In order to solve the creadox, we have developed the 'COCD box' (see 'Technique 1: The COCD box' on page 134).

Letting Go
Choosing also means letting go of other ideas that won't be developed any further. As you move on within the converging process, the choice can become more difficult and weighty. Sometimes you have to let go of concepts that have taken a lot of time and effort to come up with, in order to dedicate your attention to more promising concepts. Efficiency of choice combined with letting go is an important skill which the creative thinker will need in order to succeed in the converging phase. The training area will offer tools to reinforce this skill.

Focusing on the Differences
During the evaluation and selection of ideas we often hear, 'Oh, that idea is the same as this other idea on the list.' Both consciously and unconsciously, this expression is one of the killers of new ideas. People are rather inclined to seek out similarities because they always want to fit the new in with what they already know. The expression 'this idea looks like the other one' suggests that if it looks like the old one, it cannot be an innovative idea. Even worse, if they compare it to an old idea that didn't work, the new idea will have no chance of survival.

A trained creative thinker will always look for the differences between ideas because these differences hide the real innovative value. Sometimes a minimal difference in a concept can make a big difference to a customer if you can make the best of it. When you look at the list of ideas on page 122 you will notice that ideas 9 to 12 seem very similar. Yet all the ideas are not equally good.

Intuition

Since management guru Mintzberg emphasised the importance of intuition it has been more thoroughly studied and described as a management skill. One could define intuition as an immediate form of 'knowing' in which experience and the sixth sense are connected. It is 'choosing from the heart' and results in concentrated inspiration. Intuition ability will grow as a person gains more experience. It is important to acknowledge this, to become conscious of it and be able to recognise when and how your intuition manifests itself.

People who follow their intuition to quite a large extent can be very persistent. They also encounter difficulties in expressing (rationalising) why they have chosen something, but they 'know' that it is the right choice. Steve Jobs was very persistent when it came to his idea for the Apple operating system in spite of much opposition. The Sony chairman, Akio Morita, defended his Walkman idea against the organisation.

Selection Techniques

Now we will discuss a number of selection techniques. Some of these will be elaborately described, others will be merely mentioned. The techniques below also apply to group processes. Choosing with a group has its own patterns and challenges. However, using the COCD box is the best technique in almost all situations since it helps to reach a better understanding of your own innovative ideas and helps you to communicate them more effectively.

" OUR GREATEST GLORY IS NOT IN NEVER FALLING, BUT IN RISING EVERY TIME WE FALL Confucius

Creative Session

Choosing with groups can be divided into two different selection processes.

   A. During creative sessions, as a group participant you are invited to be at the service of the problem owner. You will of course have your own opinions but at the same time you consider the ideas from the point of view of the problem owner. You choose and develop the ideas that offer the largest added value from their perspective. This is the selection process that we will develop further in *Creativity Today*.

   B. A totally different situation is when there are elements within the group that need to take one particular standpoint (defensive) and yet a shared decision is necessary. One could call this 'selection by negotiation'. It is very common in political situations; for example, during negotiations between unions and employers. This is a political decision process. We will *not* treat that process in this book.

Choosing within groups has several procedural and psychological aspects. When selecting your 'choice model', consider the following:
   • the commitment of the group
   • the number of ideas you are starting with, and how many ideas you want to end with
   • the degree of innovation you are aiming at
   • the culture of the environment in which you will be working

Technique 1: The COCD Box®

The COCD box was created by a Dutch-Flemish organisation for the development of creative thinking – the abbreviation COCD stands for Centre of Development of Creative Thinking. The COCD box is one of the better techniques to have been developed in recent years to manage the start of the convergence phase. You can apply it to all kinds of problems and in all kinds of groups. By using the COCD box to make a selection of the most promising ideas, you can focus on real innovation and you will increase the group's emotional commitment towards the selection that has been made.

The COCD box originated from frustration at the creadox. How can we avoid falling back into old patterns and wasting innovative potential?

When selecting ideas according to the COCD box method, you consider two basic criteria. On the one hand, degree of innovativeness – is the idea old hat or new? On the other hand, feasibility: is the idea easy or difficult to realise? Feasibility should take into account costs, legality, technical feasibility, strategy, etc – in short, everything that could make you think an idea might be difficult to achieve.

Based on these two criteria – originality and ease of implementation – we get a diagram with three interesting boxes.

The COCD Box

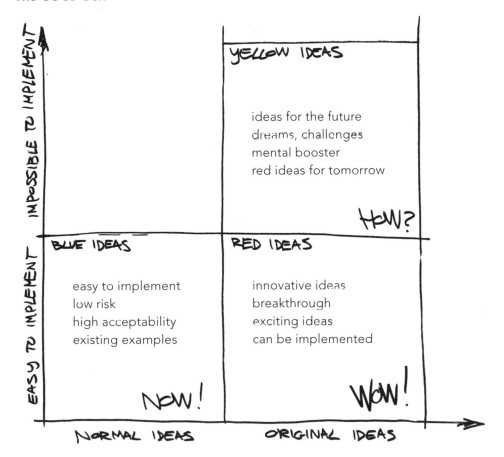

In the bottom left box we find the **blue ideas**. These are common and feasible ideas. They are very useful, there's nothing wrong with them. These ideas would probably have resulted from an ordinary meeting.

The bottom right box shows the **red ideas**. In fact, a creative session is meant to generate red ideas. The red ideas are exciting and innovative, and yet, your intuition tells you that these ideas could be realised without too much trouble.

On the top right there is a category of ideas that normally get lost at the end of almost every creative session: the **yellow ideas**. You know that these ideas are not feasible, but you find them exceptional. In a fantasy world you would go for the yellow ideas. But you have to face it, in their actual form, they cannot be achieved.

Nevertheless, this does not mean that the yellow ideas should simply be ignored. Perhaps they have just come too early. Perhaps there is no budget available now, but there could be in the future. You might not achieve them yourself but someone else might. It is worth saving these ideas for the future. Using the PMD development technique (explained later) you can find out if it is possible to transform your yellow idea into a red one.

Creative Session
How do you apply the COCD box in a creative session with a group?

The COCD box should be the first thing you use after the diverging phase. The group can use the COCD box to make a first selection from the list of ideas. It is a good idea if the ideas are written on a flip board and each one is numbered.

1. Each participant receives 7 blue, 7 red and 7 yellow dot stickers, or less if there are fewer than 100 ideas.
2. Each participant views the list of ideas and silently chooses the ones that seem best to him or her…
3. …then writes the numbers of the chosen ideas onto the (B, R, Y) stickers.
4. When everyone has done this, they place the stickers next to the appropriate ideas on the board.
5. The coach draws a large COCD box on a new sheet.
6. The best 6 to 20 ideas (for example, the ones with a minimum of 3 dots) are transferred to the appropriate quadrants according to their dominant colour.
7. Each participant has the possibility to argue for one idea that has not been chosen according to the democratic method. If there is one other person who supports him/her, the idea will be added to the others in the COCD box.
8. From now you will only consider the ideas in the COCD box and move on to the development phase.

Who's afraid of red, yellow and blue?
Barnett Newman

TIP FOR THE COACH

1. CHOOSING SILENTLY PREVENTS PARTICULAR PARTICIPANTS TAKING CONTROL
2. SEVERAL PARTICIPANTS MAY GIVE DIFFERENT COLOURS TO THE SAME IDEA. WHERE SHOULD YOU PUT IT IN THE COCD BOX?
   - THE DOMINANT COLOUR WINS
   - WITH AN EVEN NUMBER OF DOTS: BLUE TAKES PRECEDENCE OVER RED, RED OVER YELLOW
   - IN THE CASE OF 1 BLUE, 1 RED AND 1 YELLOW DOT, THIS IS A RED IDEA BECAUSE 2 PARTICIPANTS THINK IT IS FEASIBLE AND 2 THINK IT IS ORIGINAL

Communicating with Blue, Red, Yellow

We have noticed that communication about innovative ideas becomes a lot easier when all parties involved are familiar with the colour code. A listener will react differently to proposals of a different colour. When you present a blue concept, you have to make sure that the implementation plan is included. For a yellow idea, the potential should be examined first. 'How beautiful is this dream?' For a red concept, you will have to excite the listener and you know that you'll have to be more persuasive than with a blue idea.

We have already seen that one project group proposed a yellow idea to their bosses. The top managers became so enthusiastic that they tried to find all kinds of ways to achieve this concept. This is of course the situation any project team dreams of.

Let's have a look at a few more selection techniques for groups.

Technique 2: Hits per Target Group

What is it? If several groups are represented in a creative session, for instance different departments, you could give the participants of each group dot stickers of the same colour (i.e. one colour per group). Have them put the stickers next to the ideas they like best as previously. The colours will highlight the preferences of the sub-groups.

When do you use it? Use it when the commitment of several (represented) groups is very important to the development of an idea. Take product development for example, where it is really important that your production department as well as your sales and marketing departments and research & development find the idea interesting enough to pursue.

An idea on its own is nothing! As long as an idea has not been adopted by a person or a team, it has no chance of survival. Nigel MacLennan distinguishes three factors for measuring the possible success of an idea:

- the quality of the idea
- the quality of the person or the team who will realise the idea
- the degree of commitment of these people

He estimates that the third factor, commitment, is undeniably the most important factor in determining the chances of an idea's success. It is harder to achieve an outstanding idea with outstanding people who have a low level of commitment than an average idea that is realised by average people who absolutely believe in the success of the idea.

Good taste is the enemy of creativity
Pablo Picasso

Technique 3: Dr. Love

What is it? Each team-member chooses the one idea on the list that he/she is instantly attracted to. In effect, this means indicating which ideas they want to put their energy into. This choice is the starting point for the development phase in which you let people develop and realise the ideas they like the best.

When do you use it? It can be used during different phases in the process but especially when you're approaching the realisation phase. Of course, you can also combine Dr. Love with other techniques.

Selecting Creatively

You are now familiar with several selection methods for the converging phase. You will have understood that it is sometimes necessary to adapt your methods to the team, the subject and the specific conditions. Be creative in this matter. A spectacular example of this is the 'Court Day' at Heerema Infrastructures, described below.

A Day at Court
Johan Schippers, at the time project leader of the development team at Heerema Infrastructures, tells the story: 'During previous months, our team had come up with around 55 innovative concepts for tunnel construction. Now we had to choose since we could only thoroughly develop a few ideas. On the one hand, we wanted to make a radical selection, but on the other hand it was crucial to maintain the high level of enthusiasm and good atmosphere within the team because those same people would further develop the chosen concepts. This was not so easy as we had already been working on this project for about four months and during the last couple of weeks some of the guys had put all their energy into the conception and design of some very innovative (yellow) tunnel construction concepts that we might have to 'cut' now.

We decided to organise a Court Day. First, a jury (consisting of three people, including myself) would choose the most promising concepts from the 55. This shortlist was then communicated to the 16 project members. On Court Day, in the presence of the whole team, each team member had the opportunity to 'defend' a concept that had not passed the jury selection. To add a more dramatic touch to the proceedings, the judges wore real gowns and wigs. After each impassioned plea, the whole group, acting as a jury, judged if the concept would be accepted or not, using the Roman thumbs-up/ thumbs-down voting system.

After quite a turbulent meeting, around 12 ideas from the list of 55 had made it to the voting round. More importantly, thanks to the playful battle, which was of course concluded with a drink, the team were able to let go of the non-chosen concepts and go ahead with further developing the remaining concepts the following day.'

By applying one of the above-mentioned methods, you will have made your choice of which concepts to continue with. The next stage is development.

DEVELOPMENT

New Ideas are Never Immediately 'Ready to Use'

New ideas originate in the mind of the conceiver as sudden flashes during the creative process. They create an opportunity or a path towards a solution to a problem that somebody has struggled with. But they are only the starting point. We can consider the initial ideas as rough gems that still need to be polished. They only become beautiful once you add energy and increase their value.

Ideas need to evolve from an abstract, conceptual level to a concrete, practical level, otherwise they will always remain what they are: ideas. The evolutionary process requires effort and developmental skills on the part of the creative thinker but there are a number of techniques that can help him accomplish this.

The questions you should always ask yourself are, 'What stands between the current idea and its realisation? Why is it not yet available? What could prevent me from putting this into practice?'

There are several possible answers to these questions:
- the idea might be too vague
- nobody might have thought of it before
- perhaps it adds too little value to the world
- perhaps it is technically unfeasible
- or legally not possible
- there might be no real problem owner
- the added value of the idea is not obvious to the outside world
- etc.

Some of these answers are directly related to the idea itself, others to the context in which the idea will be achieved. When developing an idea, you will first need to look at the idea-specific elements. These are the aspects of the idea itself that you should improve. Afterwards you will work on the environmental factors.

In the case of an 'edible table' an idea-specific problem is that it is not stable enough. The fact that it would have to comply with food regulation standards is an environmental aspect.

Good ideas are not adopted automatically. They must be driven into practice with courageous patience

Hyman Rickover

The Development Circle

You have chosen an idea. You consider it valuable but you want to enhance it and make it stronger. The development circle is a three-step model you can apply one or more times to idea development. It enables you to create stronger ideas and ups the survival odds.

These are the three steps:
1. First you should **design** your idea carefully.
2. Secondly you will **judge** it. What is it worth? This is the judgement.
3. Next you will **enrich** the idea.

Finally you will describe it again in its enriched form.

For each of the steps in the development circle we offer several tools which have already proven their practical value. You can apply most of the techniques individually when developing your ideas. Some techniques offer more added value when applied in a group, generally during longer development processes.

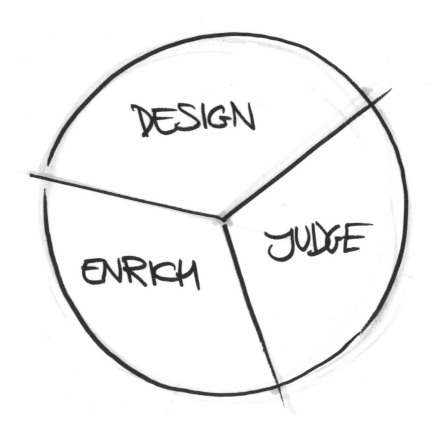

DESIGNING

The importance of a precise description of a fresh idea cannot be overestimated. By describing your idea you are imagining a new reality. You should try to imagine the idea as precisely as possible and turn it into an 'image'. By thinking the idea through and imagining it, possible shortcomings as well as new opportunities will become clearer. Furthermore, this way of handling the idea energises.

You can model an idea by describing it in words or by making a drawing or a diagram, anything that may help to clarify the idea to yourself and other people. You will find three methods of designing ideas below.

Technique 1: An Idea Form

What is it? Outline an idea on a specially devised form. Idea forms give structure to the diversity of ideas so that both judgement and development can run smoothly.

When do you use it? Idea forms are often used during creative sessions to get a better description of the ideas that have been selected.

SUBJECT *Railway strike (see page 77)*

IDEA TITLE *Advertising on the trains (yellow idea)*

DESCRIPTION

Develop a variety of advertising opportunities on the trains: publicity on tickets, in stations, in carriages, on the outside of carriages, infotainment in the trains, etc.

Advantages – offers new financial possibilities
Disadvantages – not easy to connect to our goals – politically difficult to sell

---

Technique 2: The Mirror

What is it? Express your idea to another person whose role it is to ask clarifying questions. The listener will not judge the idea and will continue to ask questions until everything is completely clear. This gives the idea's creator the opportunity of further modelling his idea during the conversation.

When do you use it? Anytime. Consider this as a way of testing an idea and refining it.

Technique 3: Cartoon

What is it? Ask a designer to draw your idea.

When do you use it? If it is affordable, it is worthwhile engaging a designer or a cartoonist during creative sessions. These professionals give form to ideas fast, and this, of course, will speed up the design process. Drawings are very motivating for the participants.

Examples
Drawings for designer case studies, see pages 118 to 120.

JUDGING

Once the idea has been described clearly, you need to ask yourself what you think of it. You will judge it. 'I like it' or 'I don't like it' is obviously not sufficient. You have to examine the idea from all angles.

It is not easy to judge innovative ideas. Sometimes this can lead to an emotional conflict – if you have come up with and designed an idea yourself, you're obviously not keen to look at its disadvantages. This means distinguishing between emotional and rational judgement.

In general during a creative process, you will need to evaluate several developed ideas. This is another reason why you should judge carefully and act efficiently at the same time.

In *Creativity Today*, we will dedicate only limited attention to the very rational selection techniques such as return-on-investment calculations, business plans, and so on because the more innovative the ideas are, the more difficult it becomes to apply traditional management methods. At this stage, innovative ideas are an unknown quantity and you might not have all of the necessary data at your disposal to apply extensive rational analysis.

This is why you need techniques that leave space for exploring, feeling and discovering their potential. Below you will find the types of assessment methods for this phase of convergence.

> 'Freedom means nothing, if it doesn't include the freedom to make mistakes.' Mahatma Ghandi

Technique 1: SePoNe (Sense, Positive, Negative)

What is it? SePoNe allows space to both feeling and rationality when judging an idea.

1. You always start by allowing your feelings free reign. This is Sensing. Caution – when you do this, you have to switch off reason. 'What kind of feeling does this idea give you?' There is no need for explanation, just describe what you feel
2. Only after you have done this, will you use reason to consider the idea. You start with the **Positive (advantages)**. 'What are the strong points of this idea?' Describe them, with comment if necessary

3. Finally you reconsider the idea, using reason again, but this time you adopt a pessimistic attitude: **Negative**. You look for the disadvantages, the flaws, the weak points. 'What does this idea lack? What can go wrong?'

Each of these three aspects has its own value. Too often the three factors are muddled up together which causes chaos. The trick is to deal with the three steps separately and successively in a fast and disciplined way.

When do you use it? For example when you want to judge a series of similar ideas. This can easily be done in a group.

Technique 2: Prefer

What is it? You judge the ideas according to 4 parameters: Potential, Risk, Effort and Feeling (=PREFer) on a simple scale ranging from 1 to 10, or low-medium-high. (Let's Prefer these ideas!)

When do you use it? When you need to make a quick selection from a large number of innovative concepts.

Example
The vertical column below indicates the concepts. Some of the 'table' ideas from the designer case study serve as an example. This table shows that the second and the fourth concept have the highest chances of success.

	Potential	Risk	Effort	Feeling	Total
Baby Box Table	3	7	8	4	5,5
Anti-Spill Table	4	8	8	6	6,5
Tea for Two	4	3	4	7	4,5
Hanging Table	8	6	5	9	7
Jumping Table	3	4	7	6	5

Technique 3: Multi-Criteria Analysis

What is it? This is a more structured and planned method of selection. You list the criteria from the original briefing and then put the most promising ideas alongside these criteria.

When do you use it? When dealing with more complex and sometimes more technically oriented selection processes or when you want to involve a larger group of people in the decision making process.

Example

The following table could be suitable for the judgement of a new product.

Criteria can be divided into:
- **black and white criteria**: where the answer is yes or no
- **gradation criteria**: where the answer is graded, e.g. from 1 to 10

Does this idea add value to our enterprise?	Criterion	Answer

Regarding Our Business

	Criterion	
1. Does this idea add something new to our business?	yes/no	
2. How big is the market potential?	in ¥ € $	
3. Is there a proven consumer need?	yes/no	
4. Does this product fit into our strategy?	1-10	
5. Is there a clearly defined target group?	yes/no	

Regarding Our Production Capacities

	Criterion	
6. Could this product harm other existing products?	yes/no	
7. Could this product use other brands to piggyback on or enhance other brands?	1-10	
8. Can we produce this product with the available production methods?	yes/no	
9. Does this product fit into our existing distribution methods?	yes/no	
10. Does this product meet our values?	1-10	

CREATIVE SESSION

NEEDLESS TO SAY YOU CAN USE MANY VARIATIONS WHILE JUDGING IDEAS. ALWAYS BEAR EFFICIENCY AND USER-FRIENDLINESS IN MIND. GROUPS USUALLY FIND JUDGING DIFFICULT SO IT CAN TAKE QUITE A WHILE. BY USING A CLEVER TOOL, YOU CAN REDUCE JUDGEMENT TIME AND MAINTAIN ENERGY WITHIN THE GROUP.

ENRICHING

Once you have judged and selected a limited number of hits from your ideas list, you need to ensure that these ideas can be a success in the outside world. You wouldn't like to see one of your brilliant ideas swept away just like that. The next stage is about enriching your ideas, making them stronger, developing them, dealing with the weak points and solving them. An enriched idea stands on its own two feet and is not easily put aside.

During this phase, some ideas might not appear as strong as you first thought and some of the disadvantages might not be as easily overcome as you had hoped. *Don't worry!* It is better to drop the idea now than later on, when you are already in the implementation phase. You still have other ideas up your sleeve.

In this enhancing phase, there are several techniques that can help to improve the quality of the process (and consequently the results).

Technique 1: PMD

What is it? The PMD method allows you to judge and enrich a large number of ideas quickly. Speed is an important factor in PMD, you stick to the most important points for each aspect. PMD stands for Plus, Minus, Develop.

P(lus):   What are the 2 or 3 most important plus points of this idea?
M(inus):   What are the 2 or 3 most important minus points of this idea?
D(evelop):   Think of ways to deal with the minuses in order to make the
             idea stronger.

When do you use it? When you want to do a quick (ten minutes per idea) enrichment exercise with a lot of ideas and/or a limited amount of time. This can lead to a second selection.

Example
A table with an inclined top
    P: easy to read on
       takes up less space
    M: objects slide down it
       you can only use it from one side
    D: you could flip it open to make a horizontal top
       make adapted plates and cutlery, add edges to the tabletop
       a double tabletop that can be folded up from the middle

THE PERSON WHO DOESN'T MAKE M

Technique 2: SCAMPER

What is it? This technique enables you focus on the different elements of your topic and ask yourself each time what you could change to make it stronger.

SCAMPER stands for:
   S: Substitute
   C: Combine
   A: Adapt
   M: Minimise/maximise
   P: Put to other use
   E: Eliminate
   R: Reverse

When do you use it? If, after judging an idea, you are still not convinced of its power and you think it can be further enhanced. You can either focus on enriching the idea by using the minuses as a point of departure, or you can work intuitively and see where this leads you.

Technique 3: All Senses

What is it? If an idea appeals to several senses at the same time, it will have greater impact. When you are enriching ideas you can try working with the different senses to add more to your idea such as features you hadn't thought of before. In this context, 'senses' can be interpreted more broadly than just the traditional five senses of touch, sight, hearing, taste and smell.

Sight	Can you improve the look of the product, adapt it, change the colours, add new angles, create another perspective…?
Hearing	Extra publicity (noise), let the idea speak for itself, use another language…
Taste	Consider the style, type of design, analyse the tastes of the target group, introduce a 'sweetener'…
Smell	Relate to pleasant or primary smells, think of intuitive reactions…
Touch	Make it more tactile, come closer to the customer…

Movement, orientation, rhythm of life etc can also be inspiring.

When do you use it? Always applicable if you want to dress up an idea.

Paul Arden

YES IS UNLIKELY TO MAKE ANYTHING

YOU HAVE TO LET PEOPLE " CHALLENGE YOUR IDEAS

Tom Kasten

> **Example**
> This is a quote from an advertising text, 'In the era of the Active
> Hedonist, Coca-Cola offers a true sensation for all our senses.
> The ice-cold bottle in your hand is the herald of a great refresh-
> ment, the typical colour a trademark of its own. The flipping
> crown cap that clears the way for the sparkling gold is a treat to
> your ears. Extracts of tropical plants titillate your nostrils irresist-
> ibly. And the unique effect of a sparkling Coca-Cola on your taste
> buds is indescribable.'

Technique 4: The Elevator Pitch

What is it? This is a well-known marketing technique applied to new concepts,
which 'forces' you to:
- Simplify your message
- Shorten your message
- Focus on your Unique Selling Proposition (USP)

All kinds of creative challenges outside the world of business can also benefit
from this kind of positioning of the message.

When do you use it? An elevator pitch is particularly useful when you don't
have much time to convince someone, and when you are in competition with
many others.

Example

An elevator pitch is often constructed as follows:
1. What is the problem/challenge/need?
2. What is the solution?
3. Why is it unique?

The USP is normally translated into one catchy slogan, strap line or pay-off:
- Virgin Express: 'Mine's Bigger Than Yours' – Written on the back
  of the Airbus A340-600s because they are the longest passenger
  aircraft in the world
- LifeStraw: 'The personal water purification tool'
- Apple: 'Think different'

Keep it simple!
When enriching ideas, we are often inclined to complicate them. This happens spontaneously because we start with a basic idea and want to keep this point of departure as intact as possible. This is perfectly justifiable.

However, it will often become clear that the basic idea is not strong enough and that the obstacles cannot be solved without some very complex constructions. This is generally a sign that you should abandon the idea.

The greatest ideas are simple ones.

Development Circle Step 4 = Step 1 Designing

You're back at the beginning of the development circle. You now need to design an enriched idea so that it is as easy as possible to communicate. You should think about the best ways of presenting your idea in order to increase its chances of success.

The designing can be undertaken in many different ways. That would depend on the idea itself and the context in which it will be presented. Try to come up with a creative presentation that also reflects the innovative power of the new idea. The medium is the message.

What might this be? Presentation, scale-model, speech, role-play, poster, report, drawing, website, interactive DVD, movie, parade, legal article, article, essay, book, dummy, post-it note, suggestion box proposal, advertising, announcement, etc.

SYNTEGRATION AT THE IDEAS LIST LEVEL

Until now, in this development phase, we have been talking about the development of the ideas themselves. You started with a series of ideas, selected the best ones, judged and enriched them. A certain number of ideas have been dropped, until only the very best ideas are left over.

Suppose, in the example of new table designs, you came up with 145 ideas and selected 14 of them. You judged and enriched them and the two most promising concepts remained. These are the ones that you have decided to execute. However, not all subjects are like this. Almost all issues that begin with 'How can we…?' will generate very unequal ideas during the diverging phase: big and small ideas, detailed ideas and vague visions, technical and organisational pointers and so on. In this case, after the selection, you will still find unequal ideas in the COCD box.

These different individual ideas may not provide the solution to your problems alone but if they are cleverly combined they can open up interesting solution-oriented views. Combining these ideas is called 'syntegrating', a mental activity crucial to superior convergence. It is important but not easy.

Definition: 'Syntegration' is the technique of combining different promising ideas within one (concept), offering a distinct overall vision of the solution to the problem.

Syntegrating goes beyond the level of enriching the individual idea. It is applied at the level of **all ideas**, the totality of ideas. It is not the same as 'clustering' which is adding several ideas together under the same description. Syntegrating means taking **different kinds** of ideas and bringing them together into a new solution-oriented concept.

> **Is this still too abstract?**
> Try this metaphor. Imagine a cook who prepares a meal using different ingredients. The dishes will be different when the cook uses other ingredients, works in another kitchen, cooks for another occasion or for other guests. There are many ways of preparing Shepherd's Pie, even with the same ingredients.
> But there is another way of cooking – he can open the refrigerator and prepare all kinds of combinations from the available ingredients. Each time, he 'syntegrates' a dish.

How do you syntegrate promising ideas? Syntegrating is more than a trick or a technique. The way it works is similar to resociation (see page 110) but you start from different points of departure at the same time: the creative thinker keeps the target in mind, overlooks the promising ideas in the COCD box and comes up with some combinations. He puts the elements together in a new and different way. Syntegrating is a skill you can improve with practise. It is undoubtedly the most difficult phase in the creative process because quite disparate ideas are combined. The creative thinker's own proficiency in this has an important bearing on the result.

Technique: The Big 4

What is it? The Big 4 is a syntegration method. The ideas in the COCD box provide your point of departure. You give yourself (or the group) the task of using these ideas as basic ingredients with which to conceive of 4 different total solutions, each with its own angle.

When do you use it? After converging the ideas.

ACTIVATION

'We have enough ideas, we need to realise them!'
Tens of thousands of ideas remain hidden in drawers, jotted on post-it notes or beer coasters, end up in action plans (or worse: on rolled-up flip-charts) after meetings, are discussed in canteens and pubs, but will never see the light of day. Only a fraction of all these beautiful, promising ideas are eventually achieved. Perhaps this is just as well. Imagine if everything anyone ever came up with was realised! Bear in mind that Darwin's law, 'the survival of the fittest', also applies to ideas.

Passion is key

An idea itself amounts to very little. Why is it that some ideas get realised and others just seen to disappear? Passion is the key! Only if someone really truly wants it will he realise an idea. The ratio of 10% inspiration to 90% transpiration applies here. Many ideas management systems fail. The reason is that we tend to disconnect the idea and the person (passion) and make it, in many cases, a combined responsibility.

Talking about realising ideas equals talking about initiatives

An idea in itself is nothing, yet combined with action it becomes an initiative. An initiative can be seen, measured and implemented.

IDEA + ACTION = INITIATIVE

You will need to convince people and motivate them to join you in realising your idea. Newness or innovation is not always welcomed with open arms. Your colleagues have their own things on their minds and some might like to keep the upper hand. The fact that you (once again) propose a new idea, might be threatening to them.

Only once the idea is finally realised (literally: has become reality) will you be able to rest, and not before then.

'Activating' means preparing for action. Activating requires:
- feeling well and thinking well
- judging the potential reactions
- determining a strategy
- assessing motivation, and if necessary increasing it
- finding helping hands
- thinking of arguments to convince colleagues, bosses, customers
- and finally, going into action: doing, running, talking, selling, phoning, motivating, convincing, moving, going…

Change always begins with that first step!

There are a certain number of methods and techniques you can use to activate ideas. We have provided just a selection and not everything is always applicable. Judge for yourself what might be useful for you, your team or your problem. Try out different methods. Good techniques are techniques that work for you.

Activation has 3 parts:
1. **Motivation.** Start with yourself or your team. First check if your own motivation level matches the goal to be achieved.
2. **Outside world.** Find out how the outside world will react to your proposal, concept, innovation and think of ways of dealing with possible resistance.
3. **Action path.** This allows you to ascertain how you can support yourself and others during the realisation.

MOTIVATION

Feeling always comes first! You have chosen the ideas with the most potential from a wide range. You have developed some of these ideas. A number of ideas have become stronger, others have been dropped. You might also have made new choices and syntegrated. You have worked on the best way of meeting the goal you had set and you are satisfied. The end is near and you can feel the energy of the promising concepts.

'Tell me and I'll forget. Show me and I might remember. Involve and I'll understand.' anonymou

But is this really true? You may be enthusiastic about the idea, but are you also motivated enough to put it into practice? Motivation is the most important factor in successfully-implemented innovation. As already described in chapter 4 (the starting phase), a powerful idea, performed by capable people, can be easily let slide if the necessary motivation and the absolute will to succeed is missing. An average idea, developed by a group of averagely qualified but highly motivated people, has a greater chance of actually being executed.

Technique 1: Visualising the Realisation
What is it?
Visualise the final result.
In this visualisation exercise, you begin with the realised idea and take a very close look at its different aspects. You experience what kind of feelings the idea evokes. Visualising helps you to access your deeper feelings and to become detached from the emotions of the moment. Work out which aspects of the idea give you energy and which ones you consider to be obstacles. Is the result more positive than negative?

Visualise the action path.
You can use this particular visualisation to gain a better picture of the action path towards realisation. You begin with the 'realised situation'. Then you visualise 'going back' step by step along the path towards realisation until you arrive at the present moment. This allows you to see which obstacles you will need to overcome in order to achieve your goal.

When do you use it? This is an extra technique that serves as a test of your commitment towards the realisation of the idea. It also provides a clearer picture of the path that leads towards the final execution.

> **Example**
> Westerners often think that the Japanese spend a seemingly endless amount of time on discussions about future projects before they actually get started. From that point of view, this is a waste of time. 'Let's get started instead of talking about it,' is a frequent remark.
>   A Dutch manager who used to work for the Mitsubishi-Volvo production department once told us that in his opinion this is one of the most fundamental differences in Japanese and European team management. He added, 'I noticed several times that the few days 'lost' at the beginning of a project were easily regained later on because we had already talked through all of the obstacles that we might have to face, before they actually materialized. There was almost always a net gain of time.'

Technique 2: Find the Opportunity Owner

What is it? The people who have conceived and developed an idea are often not the most suitable people to execute it. As a conceiver of an idea you are often expected to take care of its realisation which might not be quite what you had in mind. If this happens regularly, you will end up refraining from coming up with new ideas.

'Find the opportunity owner' means finding who within the organisation (or outside of it) is the best person to realise this idea. Look at the values, intrinsic motivation, personal ambition, timing, and personal capabilities required.

When do you use it? In the transition from the creative phase to the innovation or implementation phase.

OUTSIDE WORLD

Any change that you initiate will destabilise your environment. Change is like a pebble thrown into a pond – the area of water the pebble hits will ripple. The further the distance from the 'centre', the fewer ripples you will see.

However, there is no such thing as a motionless pond; other people are also throwing pebbles into the water. Your project is only part of this complex game. It is really worthwhile to take the time to examine the pond, observe it carefully and judge the surface tension you are about to enter.

You should also realise that your view of the topic will have changed fundamentally. During and due to the previous steps in the creative process, both your vision and your sensitivity will have altered. You can now see opportunities and solutions that you hadn't been aware of before. Don't forget, though, that for the people around you, nothing has changed.

Long Live Resistance! Don't assume that resistance is bad. On the contrary, if you don't encounter any resistance when you introduce a new product or innovation, you're probably not dealing with anything very important. Resistance is useful. Use your opponents as consultants – they represent (and defend) the values that (as they see it) are attacked by the innovation. Resistance is always interesting; it may show that you have misjudged something or simply that you should communicate differently.

Technique 1: Resistance Analysis and Value Response
What is it?
- Ascertain what kind of resistance you experience when selling or applying an innovation. Sometimes this is very explicit and clear, sometimes obscure. Listen as carefully as possible
- Find out what kind of values are behind this resistance
- Formulate your response based on the values, not the resistance

When do you use it? If it is obvious that changes generate hypersensitive reactions from certain parties.

Technique 2: Energisers and Resisters
What are they?
- **Energisers** support you and generate energy to keep things running. Everything that can be used to accelerate realisation is an energiser. What can you draw energy from? Who would like to help you?
- **Resisters** are all the factors in your environment and within yourself that can block realisation. Which things do you dread the most? Who will oppose you and why?

Perform a divergence exercise on energisers and resisters relating to your idea. Make a list. Bear them in mind and use them when you describe your path of action.

When do you use them? Before you describe your path of action.

Example
Energisers can be: people, presentations, means, encouragement, customers, test teams, structures, values, finance…

Resisters can be: people, (lack of) means, structures, laws, agreements, habits, values…

ACTION PATH
Once the outside world has been mapped, you can draw up your action path. The traditional way of doing this is by writing an action plan. This will at the very least state **who** will do **what** and **when**. There are also newer ways of describing your action path.

Technique 1: Want/Do matrix
What is it?

	I do / I don't want to	I do / I want to
Do	Decrease	Keep
	Say goodbye	Enjoy
	Delegate	Intensify
Don't do	I don't do / I don't want to	I don't do / I want to
	Accept	Create
	Communicate	Develop
	Say no	Invest
	Don't want to	**Want to**

A lack of time is the most important failure factor in terms of innovation. Another important factor is priority. New ideas have to be realised alongside other activities. The Want/Do matrix is a powerful tool for change, both on the strategic organisational level and on level of personal action. It is an easy way of considering the use of your means (time, money, attention) and it offers an insight into what you will have to do and especially what you will have to omit in order to bring about change.

How does it work? You start by visualising the final result. You then consider what you have to change in your current activities in order to make this possible.

In the **top right-hand square** you write down what you are doing now and which things you want to keep doing. What are you satisfied with? The aim of this activity is to improve present quality where possible, but more particularly to continue with and to profit from it. This quadrant ensures the continuity of important projects.

Top left you write down what you are doing now but have to stop doing in order to achieve the goal in mind. You will say goodbye, learn to say no to or delegate these activities. This is how you create space for change.

Bottom left you write the things you are not doing and would like to keep this way in the new context. It is important to communicate this clearly and to continue to say no when asked.

Bottom right you write down what you aren't doing yet but will need to take on in order to achieve the desired goal. This is the space for development, investment and innovation.

When do you use it? You apply the Want/Do matrix when you are considering the realisation of the solution that you would like to put in place (at the end of the converging phase). The matrix enables you to look at the innovation in a broader perspective and to fit it into the wide range of activities currently taking place. Furthermore, the Want/Do matrix is a strategic tool which can tell you which aspects should be continued, and which ones should be dropped or further developed.

Example
Here is a hypothetical example about a tri-athlete who is preparing for success at the coming world championship.

I DO / I DON'T WANT TO	I DO / I WANT TO
Social activities Keep statistics Association meetings Worry about sponsorship	Daily training schedule Look after my own equipment Take my children to school Win competitions

I DON'T DO / I DON'T WANT TO	I DON'T DO / I WANT TO
Barbecues Official appearances	Analyse competitors' results Special swimming speed training Weekly contact with supporters Train together with British competitor

Technique 2: Buddy Test

What is it? A buddy can help you on many occasions during your journey towards realisation. Choose a person who is different enough from you to be able to act as a real sparring partner. This person might have a purely advisory role or be more active. It has been proved that working in pairs is a good combination for getting innovative results.

When do you use it? You might call on your buddy as a guinea pig for your ideas, as an energiser when the going gets tough, as an alarm clock when you forget your deadlines, as a sounding board for your visions, as your go-between for the outside world, and so on.

> **Example**
> One often hears the saying, 'Behind every great man there's a strong woman.' The history of politics, science and art provides many examples of this but on an even greater number of occasions this kind of partnership remains discrete. Marriage is an institutionalised 'buddy-ship'.

Creativity is letting go

Ramon Vullings

In a pitch-dark room there's a box with 5 pairs of red socks and 4 pairs of blue socks. How many socks do you have to take out of the box to be sure that you have one proper pair?

Ten glasses stand in one straight line. The first 5 glasses are filled with liquid, the next 5 are empty. How do you make a straight line of alternating full and empty glasses when you're only allowed to move a maximum of 2 glasses?

SULPHUR DIOXIDE

Turn this page upside down in front of a mirror.
The word 'sulphur' is upside down.
What happens to the word 'dioxide'?

Innovation Breakers

Analyse until you understand everything – Follow the rules – When in do
advice of experts in the business – Hang on to what you have, then yo
and definitely – Don't question yourself or your convictions – Every
even if he is wrong – If someone has a good idea, make him do it. If
with new ones – Ignore people who are against your idea – Make a lo
time. Don't run ahead, then you won't fall – If someone proposes so
when you're absolutely sure – Don't accept your existing products be
– Never admit that you are wrong – Lay back and relax. Things will ha
– If you are good at something, keep doing it for the rest of your life
you don't like, think about going on strike – Choose the safe way – E
– Think of your own position and react when it is in danger – If some
due to you – Always do what you're asked to do – Let people expe
they will find the time for it – Don't think too much about the thing
mistakes of others – Avoid everything that could disturb your peace o

n't do it – Be happy if there is little opposition to your plans – Follow the
loose it! – Hide in the group, that's the safe way – React immediately
 see a new opportunity, grab it – Be on good terms with your boss,
any good ideas, let him do all of them. He will soon stop coming up
 career plan and stick to it – Just a reaction will do, you have enough
new, make a fool of him – If he does try, sabotage it – Continue only
n by your own new product – Look for a safe environment to work in
tick to what you know – Don't support intelligent people around you
do further training, you already know enough – If there is something
 many horses as you can – Distrust changes. They only cause trouble
 kick him again – If you don't understand something, it can never be
ith new ideas outside their regular job. If they are really motivated,
doing – Never let yourself be judged by subordinates – Enlarge the
Protect what you have – Know that you always have right on your side

THE CONVERGING PHASE

Focusing

Why do it? By focusing, you can make your target concrete and activate your concentration and energy. You should focus during the starting phase but it is also valuable right after the diverging phase. It offers a way of getting back in touch with your goal.

How do you do it? Think of your goal. What was it? Why did you consider this subject important and do you still agree that it is? What are your feelings about it? Concentrate on the target.

Exercises !

Make a list of both the interesting and uninteresting activities or conversations you did or had over the past two days. Ask yourself each time, 'What was my goal in doing this?'

Look at the ideas list for the railway case study (see pages 121 to 127) and pinpoint those ideas which focus on something other than the initial question at the start of the diverging phase.

Exercises !!!

Think of something concrete that you would like to see achieved before the end of next month. Visualise this as if it had already been realised. Bring in as many senses as you can.

Think of between three and five of the biggest challenges that your company is faced with. Convert them into a number of 'How can we…?' questions. (Tips for asking questions can be found on page 66.)

Fill in the Want/Do matrix on page 156 for yourself. Look at things that matter to you now. Express each subject as a 'How can I…?' question.

Dealing with Abundance

Why do it? Choosing is not always easy. After the diverging phase you will have an abundance of ideas of a totally different kind. This overdose of information might be paralysing. Very often there is no objective data available to help you make your choice.

How do you do it? Focus on your target. Think of the most important criteria (explicit or implicit, depending on your own style). Trust your intuition. Now consider each idea in turn and make an intuitive selection of everything that appeals to you, keeping the target in mind. Think in terms of opportunity and dare to follow your instincts.

Exercises !

Go to the library and choose a good book in less than 5 minutes.

Enter a newsagents shop. Quickly and intuitively buy a magazine that you have never read before. Read it and then ask yourself why you chose that one.

List 10 objects, people or organisations. For example: cars, flowers, male or female movie stars, novels, companies, etc. Consider them one by one and find something that makes each item on the list unique.

Exercises !!!

Take a look at the ideas list on pages 122 to 127. Cluster these ideas in 3 different ways. This will help to better assess the totality and the diversity of the ideas.

Make a list of the criteria of the toothbrush case study on page 75. Which criteria would you apply when selecting the best ideas?

Letting Go

Why do this? Converging is both choosing and at the same time letting go of something. You can only move forward if you let go of the other options when choosing an idea. Learn to accept your choice and experience satisfaction in it. This way you can fully dedicate yourself to your chosen idea and to achieving it. Letting go generates energy. Keeping hold takes up energy.

How do you do it? Letting go is a skill that can be learned. You already do it naturally by refocusing your attention time and time again. Here however, it is about letting go of something that attracts your attention, fascinates or irritates you. The stronger the emotional involvement, the more difficult it is to let go. Compare the mental act of letting go of something to relaxing a muscle after tightening it for a moment. You can do the same with a subject. Concentrate on it for a moment and then let go.

Exercises !

This is a physical relaxation exercise. Sit upright in a chair with your feet flat on the ground. Close your eyes and relax your breathing. Clench your fists and let go again. Close your eyes very firmly and relax again. Feel the difference each time. Now you can try this with every muscle in your body, feel where the tension is, and relax again. Think of something that has irritated you today. Explore this in your imagination. Take your time. Now consider the event with a smile and let go of it.

Exercises !!!

Make a list of the activities you still do but in fact shouldn't have to anymore (See the top left of the Want/Do matrix on page 155). Choose two activities from the list, one important one and one that you can easily stop. Organise saying goodbye to these activities.

Write down three important things that you want to achieve over the coming year. Now choose the most difficult one. Write down what holds you back from its realisation. Which elements in your behaviour or your character prevent you from taking the necessary steps towards the achievement of this action? Concentrate on the most important obstacles and let go of them, one by one.

Think of something you would very much like to receive from someone else but which you never seem to get. Explore this idea with a smile. Take your time. Let go of the feeling and see what happens in the weeks to come.

Syntegrating

Why do this? Individual ideas are often not powerful enough to offer a total solution to your problem. Syntegrating means combining several promising ideas into one solution-oriented concept.

How do you do it? Syntegrating works on the level of both content and design. You add different elements together in order to create something new.

Exercises !

Write a short story (around 10 sentences), include a message and use the three following words:

Grapes   Nouveau riche   Laura

Start with the following 'pairs' and combine both elements until you obtain something new. You don't have to 'end up' anywhere. Just let your imagination run freely.

shoe size	and	computer software
horticulture	and	Star Wars
invoice	and	thyroid gland
Aztec culture	and	collision

First choose 5 different objects from the room you are in. Bring them near to you if you can, or simply make a list of them. Now combine the objects in such a way as to collectively convey a (new) message, symbolise or represent something.

Exercises !!!

Return again to the ideas list for the railway case study (see page 122). Select 3 ideas at random). Syntegrate these ideas into one new stronger idea. Repeat this twice using 3 different ideas each time.

Select the best idea of the 3 you have come up with and apply PMD to it (for an explanation of PMD see page 146).

Decisiveness

Why use it? Many clever ideas settle in the heads of their conceivers but never leave the nest, brilliant concepts remain paper tigers in the drawers of creative managers. A creative thinker will only be successful if a certain number of ideas actually happen. Success is the result of a succession of daily actions. From idea to action, from word to deed! Practising decisiveness can make all the difference.

How to use it? There is no magic potion. Decisiveness is about getting started, doing something, taking action. The will is a muscle that you can develop like any other. Spring into action. Do it, NOW!

Exercise !

What should you be doing today that you have postponed for one reason or another? Why don't you put *Creativity Today* down and do this task first? How does it feel? Put the book down. Lie on your back, bend your knees and do 25 sit-ups.

Exercises !!!

Make a short list of what you consider important in life. Take one of the subjects from the top of the list and think of some new things to do that could improve this subject or field. Do one of these things before the week is out.

This is an old Buddhist willpower exercise. Think of something that you don't like but that would do you good. Do it every day for two weeks. You don't have to do it any longer than that, but keep doing it for two weeks, once a day, in a disciplined manner. It might look simple, but it works.

Have a conversation with someone who knows you well. Ask the other person what they think the most important reasons for your inaction are. Consider the top 2. Do you want to do something about it?

Practising Having Guts

'Maintaining Innovative Skills'
Why do this? As many items in this book show, you must dare to leave fixed patterns behind in order to start something new. Young people exercise this ability every day but innovating is something you lose the hang of. Trying something new is always a little frightening and this makes it a skill that you should train on a regular basis.

How do you do it? By just doing it! You can only practise innovating by doing something new every now and then.

Exercises !

Stand up immediately and do something you would never normally do in this environment. Do you feel uncomfortable? Fine. That is exactly the purpose of the exercise.

Go and see a person who you have never talked to or who you haven't seen for a long time. Have a short conversation.

Have a conversation with someone from a younger generation and find out which game or activity is very trendy in their peer group. Try it out, even if you only do it once.

Exercises !!!

Try out a new hobby within the next month or attend a meeting or event that you have never been to before.

About what in your life have you always said, 'One day I would like to...'? Make a (short) list first of all. Then choose something that cannot easily be achieved but that you would really like to do. Discuss it with your partner, family or colleagues and ask them to be supportive. Draw up a path of action and achieve your goal within a year.

Create a separate space in your diary for 'new activities', or hang a poster in a communal area. Each time you see or hear about something new, fun or tempting, write it down in the appropriate space. Agree with your family or colleagues to try something from the list, for example, twice a year.

"MAKING MYSTAKES IS ALOWED

Igor Byttebier

Developing Your Intuition

Why do it? When making choices during a creative or innovative project, logic is often side-lined because of an insufficiency of facts. The more innovative the ideas, the less information available. Intuition, knowing 'from the heart', is very useful in this kind of situation. Intuition can be worked on.

How do you do it? Being open to intuition means being receptive to information from within and learning to trust it. You have acquired this knowledge consciously and unconsciously over time. Using your intuition effectively is about learning how to connect with it . You can speed up the learning process by paying attention to your intuition: acknowledge, recognise, become conscious, apply.

In selection processes, the question, 'Will I be satisfied then?' can give an interesting indication of whether the choice is good or not. Recognising a deep and balanced feeling of satisfaction is important when it comes to making choices.

Exercises !

Try to work out how you pick up on information from within. Is it through images, words, music, colours, warmth?

In the next conversation you have, don't take notice of the contents so much as the feeling the conversation evokes. Express this feeling in a few words.

Think about something that you will do within the next hour and know you will be satisfied with. Explore this feeling of satisfaction.

Exercises !!!

Pick someone from your immediate surroundings, a person you know (or think) lives very intuitively. Find this person and start a conversation on the subject. And learn.

Consider your own life and think about those moments when your intuition positively contributed to important choices you made.

The COCD Box

Why use it? During the diverging phase you will have generated a list of ideas from which you can and must choose. The COCD box gives you the opportunity to take different kinds of ideas to the converging phase. Common sense ideas, innovative ideas and dream ideas all find their place in the COCD box. Furthermore, the COCD box colours – blue, red and yellow – allow you to communicate more easily and clearly about innovative ideas.

How do you use it? See the extensive explanation on page 134.

Exercise !

Look at the list of ideas from the railway case study (see pages 122 to 127). After reading the briefing on page 121, select the best 'blue', 'red' and 'yellow' ideas.

At the end of this section, you will find the ideas selected by the actual creative team.

Start using blue, red and yellow labels in your conversations about new ideas and concepts.

Exercises !!!

In order to really experience and practise converging you need to work with real ideas. Preferably, you will work with a list of ideas for a concrete problem, conceived by yourself or with a group. You can use the COCD box and several other techniques for these ideas.

If you have not yet applied a diverging technique to one of your own problems, we would advise you to work on one of the designer case studies from pages 74 to 76. These provide an ideal starting point for your own converging phase.

IT'S NOT IMPOSSIBLE, IT JUST HAS NEVER BEEN DONE BEFORE

anonymous

TODAY   CATEGORY Designer case study

SUBJECT Tables

ASSIGNMENT Design original tables

COCD BOX

You will find on the following pages a number of COCD box ideas taken from designers case studies as conceived by different groups on different creativity courses. They can serve as a source of inspiration and as prime material for development techniques.

YELLOW IDEAS

Air Power Table

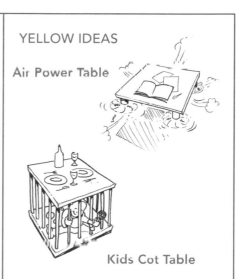

Kids Cot Table

BLUE IDEAS

'Going-up' Table

Giraffe Table

RED IDEAS

Hanging Table

Playground Table

TODAY   CATEGORY Designer case study

SUBJECT Toothbrushes

DESCRIPTION Design new toothbrushes

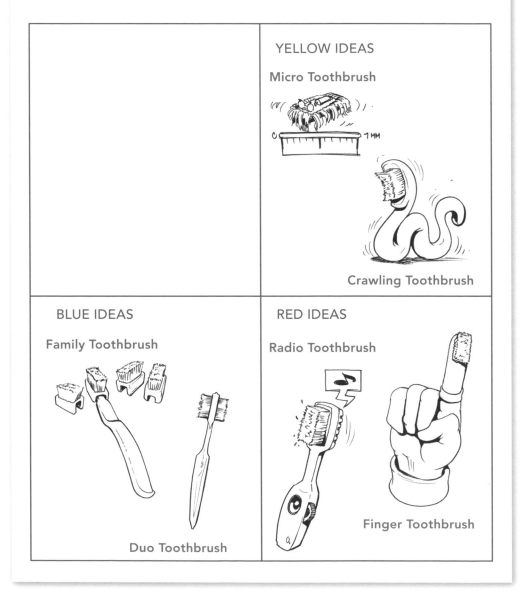

YELLOW IDEAS

Micro Toothbrush

Crawling Toothbrush

BLUE IDEAS

Family Toothbrush

Duo Toothbrush

RED IDEAS

Radio Toothbrush

Finger Toothbrush

TODAY   CATEGORY Designer case study

SUBJECT Bridges

DESCRIPTION Come up with a new bridge concept

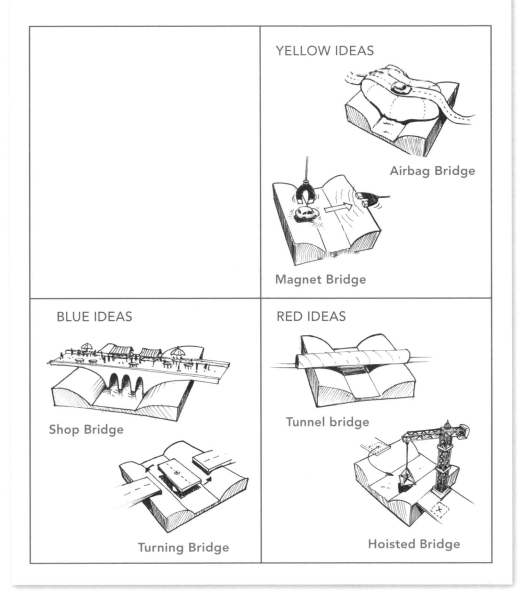

YELLOW IDEAS

Airbag Bridge

Magnet Bridge

BLUE IDEAS

Shop Bridge

Turning Bridge

RED IDEAS

Tunnel bridge

Hoisted Bridge

TODAY   CATEGORY Organisation case study

SUBJECT Railway strike

DESCRIPTION Think of alternatives

COCD box
The ideas listed below were selected by a creative group from the ideas list on pages 122 to 127.

Question: How can we strongly insure that management takes our wishes into account while we still gain the public's sympathy?

Blue ideas
5. Train the staff to have discussions around the subject with the passengers
46. Have the management travel on the trains so they can see for themselves what the restructuring means
55. Apply the restructuring activities virtually. (For example: if station X would close, hang banners in station X with the text, 'If the management applies the restructuring, the train will no longer stop here.)

TODAY   CATEGORY Organisation case study

SUBJECT Railway strike

DESCRIPTION Think of alternatives

COCD box

Red ideas
134. A free 'après-train' bar run by the train conductor's family and friends
155. Ironing on trains / in stations. Passengers could, for a fee, deliver their laundry in the morning and collect it the same evening. This concept would be franchised to the conductors so they could earn some extra money.
103. Provide a 'services train'. Equip a train with everything possibly needed during the journey. Passengers could visit a hairdresser, enjoy a pedicure, language lessons, etc. This way the passenger can make optimal use of the travel time. The railway would also have an additional source of income (based on a franchise model).
195. Humorous train hijack. Take a couple of passengers travelling on a Friday to a nice resort for a food & drink event. The press would be notified beforehand.

TODAY   CATEGORY *Organisation case study*

SUBJECT *Railway strike*

DESCRIPTION *Think of alternatives*

COCD box

Yellow ideas

56. Take away the senior management's cars and make a TV documentary about they way they cope with travelling by train instead (the delays, time table changes, etc). The camera crew would follow them on their travels for a month.

69. The railways could organise various large audience events and provides special day tickets to these events. The train conductors would be allowed to spend part of their time organising these events and they would also get a share of the profits from the events.

70. Create concept trains (party trains, cinema trains, shopping trains, etc) and implement job rotation for the train conductors. This would also generate new passenger target groups.

136. A strike lottery. In partnership with the national lottery a lottery number would be printed on every train ticket. The day after the strike – in a live TV show – the winning number would be drawn and a big prize awarded. The railway company and the national lottery company would split the costs.

TODAY   CATEGORY Convergence

SUBJECT Your own opportunities

DESCRIPTION Convergence to COCD box

	YELLOW IDEAS
Write down the best ideas from your own case studies in this COCD box. These ideas can then be developed further and syntegrated into solution-oriented concepts using the techniques on the following pages.	**HOW!**
BLUE IDEAS	RED IDEAS
NOW!	**WOW!**

The Development Circle

Why? With the development circle you can strengthen ideas until they become developed concepts that can survive in the outside world.

Exercises !

Designing
Choose an attractive idea from one of the COCD boxes on the previous pages and make an idea form yourself.

Have a 'mirror conversation' with a friend or a colleague about an idea that one of you would like to develop. You learn the most when you play the part of 'the mirror' for somebody else. The way you formulate your questions can determine the success of the process.

Judging
Choose an idea from a designer case study and judge it using SePoNe.

Multi-criteria analysis: Write down the criteria you think most relevant to one of the designer case studies. Judge the three ideas according to these criteria. Which idea is the best?

Enriching
Choose a few ideas from the COCD boxes on the previous pages and apply the following enrichment tools:
- PMD
- SCAMPER
- All Senses
- Elevator Pitch

Syntegrating
Look at the list of selected ideas from the railway case study on pages 172 to 174 or work with your own ideas. Create two different total solutions to the situation. For the first solution choose a playful point of view, for the other choose something more 'hard line'.

LIFE IS PRETTY SIMPLE:
You do some stuff. Most fails. Some works. You do more of what works. If it works big, others quickly copy it. Then you do something else. The trick is the doing something else

Leonardo da Vinci

NEARLING?

FAILURE?

SUCCESS?

NEARLING!

THE NEARLING...

is a new word for something new, undertaken with the right intentions but which has not (yet) led to the desired result.

> "I HAVEN'T FAILED,
> I'VE FOUND 10,000 WAYS THAT DON'T WORK
> Thomas A. Edison

Every time you are creating something new, you need to try, test, gamble, check, and challenge. In many cases you don't succeed (right away). You have to go through all this to gain the experience and determination to keep doing it until it works.

You're using creativity to go from 'Best Practices' to 'Next Practices'. Best practices work very well when you're transferring existing successful products, services or processes into another situation. Yet when you really want to innovate you need to go where no one has gone before and where you can't 'copy & paste' best practices. That's when the journey starts for 'Next Practices'. Looking for totally new ways of doing things will generate a lot of non-successes; these are not failures as long as you recognise them and you learn from them. The nearling sits right between failure and success.

The reasons for nearlings not to succeed can be very diverse. Perhaps the circumstances changed – a better option was chosen – you made a mistake – fate decided differently the technology – wasn't suitable yet people – weren't used to the idea yet – other priorities arose – the time wasn't right yet...

You only recognise a nearling when you look back, and you can always learn from a nearling.

You can be proud of nearlings because:
1. You started an initiative
2. You may have moved others
3. Maybe it led you to something that was successful
4. You need many nearlings, for a few successes
5. You learned from it
6. ...

The nearling emphasises that initiatives are almost ALWAYS valuable, even if they don't lead to the right result.

The nearling fills a gap in the language of international innovation.
Let's use this word.
Be inspired by others and share your own nearlings at www.nearling.com

Activating

Why do this? Conceiving and developing ideas are one aspect of creativity but as long as you don't do anything with your idea, it remains just an idea. The activation tools help you to design your path of action and increase your idea's chances of success.

How do you do this? You can apply these tools to topics from your own life or environment. Apply one of the following methods and find out what best suits you.

Exercise !

Apply the methods below to a simple task that you have to do soon, for example, think of someone you have to convince about something, a proposal you want to make, a change that you would like to introduce at work or home.

Exercises !!!

Now is the time to put the seal on the assignments you set yourself while reading *Creativity Today*. Choose the techniques among the following which are relevant to your particular tasks.

Choose an idea you would like to realise over the coming weeks. Visualise it as if it were already achieved.

Undertake a resistance analysis of the change you would like to introduce. Try to discover the values that lie hidden behind the resistance. Bear these values in mind when you conceive and express your idea.

Make a list of energisers and resisters who will play a part in the realisation of your idea.

Compose a Want/Do matrix for yourself so that putting your idea into practice is integrated into your future activities.

Choose a buddy for the realisation of your idea. Organise a meeting and remember that the energy should come from both sides.

Good luck with implementing your ideas.

Share your experiences and read about other people's experiences, find tools and tips on: www.creativitytoday.net

EVAPORATE
THEY
REALITY
INTO
MASSAGED
ARE
IDEAS
UNLESS

Alan Fletcher

CREATIVITY TODAYCEATIVIT
IVITYTODAREAYCAREATIVIT
VITYTODARYCTEATIVIYTODA
IVITYTOYCTITEAIVYTODARY
TODRYCTIATEOAIVYTDRYCT
DRYCIDVTIATEDOATRYYCYT
TYYCIDOVTIRATEDATYYCYI
AYCATYIOVTIRATEDYCATEYI
AATEYIOVTIRDTYCRAATEYIO
RTVTITAEIOAYCYDRTVTAITA
TVTAITIOYCVAEYDRTTAITIO
AREATYCTVAOEYDRTAITIYC
REAYCVTAOEYRTAIDTIYCTV
IYCNTAOEYORTAIDIYCNAOE
YCATIVITYTODAREYCNYAOE
YAOEIEVRTNADIY

ODARYCATIVITYTODAREYCT
ODYCATIVITYTODAREYCEATI
CITEATIVYTODARYCDAREAT
IATEAIVYCODAREATIVITYTY
AREATIVITYYCVTIATEOAIYT
AREATIVITYCIDVTIRATEDOA
VTIRATEATYCTYIOVTIRATED
TIRATDYCATEYIOVTIRDATYC
IDTYCRATEYIOVTAIDTYCYD
YCEYDRTVTAITAIOYCAEYDR
TVAEYDRTAITIOYCIVITYTOD
AOEYRTAIDTIYCTIVITYTODA
EYRTAIDIYCTTAOEYORTAID
ORTAIDIYCNYAOEEORTAIDI
RTADIYCNYAOEIEVRTADIYC

IEDERTNYCAIAOTEDROTVYC
NYCTDOAIAOTERNYCTTDOA
TDOAIAOYYCORTETDOAIANY
ATYCIAORNTETDOAYCRIAEC
RAENTTIOADYCORAENTTIO
ODRAYCTVOAETIODRAYCRTN
RATNOETDAIOYCRANTOETD
ATDEOIYCREAANTTODIOYC
IYCOREAINATTODYCTOREAI
RANATOIDYCEATORANTOIDY
IDYCNEAATOORTIDYCRNEA
ANATOOTIDYCREANATOTIO
TODYCRDEATINAOTOYCRDE
EDAOATINOTYCREAOATINO
OTDAYCARETIONTODAYCAR

CAIYAOEIDERTNYCAIYA

IAOTEROTNYCTDAIAOTERO

ERNYCTETDOAIAORNYCRTE

ORTETDOIANYCIAORTETDO

TOADYCRAEONTTIOADYCO

COAENTTIODRAYCVOAETTI

ETIODAYCRTNOAETODAIYC

YCRANTOAETDIOYCRANTO

EAANTTODIYCOREANATTOD

TODYCETORAINATODYCETO

ATOORANTIDYCNEATOORAT

OTIDYCRANEATOOTIDYCRE

REATNAOTIODYCREATINAO

INAOTYCRDAEOATINOTYCR

CREAATIONOTDYCREATION

NTODEAYCREATION TODAY

creation
TODAY

CREATION TODAY

In Creation Today you will be looking at creativity from a different angle. We are going to dig into organisational creativity. How do organisations change and evolve? How do we create new organisational realities?

We will explore creation and organisational development from the viewpoint that only one thing about reality is real: it is changing every instant. And we are all co-creators of this new reality.

We invite you to come along with us and find out what this vision has in store for you. Examine the consequences. Explore the possibilities.

Some real-life cases will provide you with concrete examples of how this view of creation and change works in practise. And beware! Don't view the examples as models to copy. Because if there is only one thing that sticks with you after reading Creation Today, we hope it's that you feel you are the original creator of your own reality, right here and now.

Words like love, authenticity, connection, dreams, silence, opening up, trust, and soul will be part of this exploration. Open up and go with the flow!

Godelieve Spaas & Igor Byttebier

THE WORLD IS IN MOTION

More and more studies are concluding that all things – from the infinitely small to the infinitely big – are in motion ... nothing ever rests. Stability, stillness is an illusion. Einstein claimed we should perceive motion as the natural and real state of matter, a state that we do not have to explain because it stems from the nature of the universe itself. It is the essence of existence.

Man has looked at motion in many a different way throughout the ages. Motion is often associated with things tangible: the movement of people, objects, the sun and the moon, the trees in the wind, etc. We also use the term motion as a metaphor for the development of people, companies, evolution; in short, everything that is alive, exists or could exist. Motion can be regarded as the opposite of stagnation, a phenomenon that can be started and stopped, an initiative of mankind, nature, or of the universe itself. However we can also regard motion as implicit, and as such motion is a wholeness of which everything and everyone is a part, and in which everything and everyone influences the interactions between the various motions – sometimes as a conscious and targeted action, sometimes unconsciously. This creates a continuous flow of motions that influence each other. It is the slowness of the movement or the invisibility of its direction that makes us experience motion as stagnation or stability.

The deeper meaning attributed to motion varies, too. In Western cultures, motion is almost always additive; it increases, accumulates. One thing leads to another, meaning that you first have to take one step before you can take the next. This makes motion targeted, focused, less free. Focus is always exclusive, enabling one to concentrate on part of the whole. It is not the whole that is leading, but only a fragment of the whole. By concentrating on part of the whole, we gain insight into the relationships between the parts, but not into the coherent whole.

Zooming in from an additive paradigm creates a pattern of exclusion. The emphasis on increasingly smaller things is then amplified. This results in the exclusion of more and more things and creates a more fragmented reality.

A process of inclusion is needed to gain insight into the coherent whole. The predominantly Western meaning attributed to motion is only one of many. Interpreting this meaning more loosely creates room for perceiving motion from a different angle.

Not that which exists, but that which is possible, is the starting point. Not characterising motion as an additive process but assigning it a random or rampant nature creates room for inclusion. The dynamics of inclusion embraces new impulses, freely combines all kinds of fragments with each other and responds to what happens, without a predetermined focus created by sequentiality.

Experiencing motion as a constant increases our awareness of all kinds of motion. One sees more motions and recognises more variation between the motions. The dynamics of inclusion creates more freedom to play with variation in the whole of motion.

VARIATION AND INCLUSION

Since Motion is continuous and not necessarily additive, the world is created through a continuous flow of motions that encounter each other and result in something different. Each encounter influences that which exists, purposely or accidentally. Each motion, tangible and intangible – a gust of wind, a fleeting thought, a bold decision, a growing tree – everything interacts with Motion. Depending on the observer, things may or may not appear to be coherent. The cohesion the observer wishes to associate with a variety of motions can come from within or from an outside context.

The combined action between motions is a process that starts with inclusion. Everything and everyone is allowed to participate – must participate, even. Every new creation (act, thought, shape) is included in the same ensemble.

Motion is a constant process, the result of different kinds of interactions between motions, which may, or may not, take shape: Shapes that are not amassed and hence destined to becoming stagnant. Shapes that are transient and free. Shapes that keep changing because they are not exclusive.

Some shapes last longer than a human lifetime, others only last a fraction of a second.

Motion is thus a constant and integral part of our existence in which each event and action creates and influences the whole. Sometimes something new is created; at one time, together with that which already exists, at another time, independently of that which exists. And all the little creations find their way, and together form new combinations that lead to the next transient combination of motion.

ORGANISATIONS PLAYING

Moving away from the additive meaning of motion and experiencing motion as continuous creates room for perceiving and acting differently in organisations. The focal point and starting point for organisational development is not that which exists, but that which is possible. This perspective provides an opening for creation not restricted by existing reality. It detects opportunities to forge relationships other than with history only. It enables us to take major leaps, to link seemingly incoherent worlds, to create without obstacles and expectations, and without excluding anything.

Fundamentally changing the way we experience Motion and the meaning we give it creates an open, multiform and dynamic way for companies to develop.

Most organisations consider evolution as being a series of sequential developments. One development leads to the next and each development in itself is fertile ground for the next. Organisations are in constant search for the next step up on their ladder of development. Always better, more accurate, and better thought-out, but always along the same line, thus fixing all that exists and excluding something totally different.

A number of organisations find themselves striving for predictability and reliability. The developmental process is then characterised by learning from other organisations, using proven organisational models and structured step-by-step plans – very common ways to create successful businesses. Handing over that which was is then, of course, a prerequisite. And a hand-over requires language, which means that organisations limit themselves to thinking and acting in the explicit, the known, the material, everything which can be expressed in words, arguments, plans and models.

IMPLICIT PROCESS

Underneath the explicit and conscious organisational development process, there is obviously also an unconscious and implicit process that develops the organisation. There are motions, feelings, emotions, dreams, fantasies, images, confusion and a lot more. The fact that we cannot immediately put this process into words does not mean it is not there.

And it is especially in the implicit that the spontaneity of an organisation can be found, due to an absence of shapes, focus, coagulation. When consciously including the implicit in the developmental process of an organisation, one creates room for perception alongside thought, letting things happen alongside getting things done, imagination alongside translation, floating alongside direction, paying attention to broad vision alongside paying attention to detail, feelings alongside knowledge, allowing fantasy alongside holding on to reality, experimenting alongside applying your skills.

All the dreams, fantasies, wishes, values, hopes… contribute to growth, give new life, create new angles and perspectives. In fact, especially the disparate, open and implicit images, that do not originate from that which already is or has already been determined, will contribute to an organisation's organic and continuous unfolding.

If development is continuous and not additive, then every road map, shape, method or model is merely a source of inspiration. They are nothing more than one of the many shapes that drop in, participate in the interaction and then change or disappear.

And that's exactly what this is about. How can we, in our professional activities, deal with everything that is handed to us, everything that we look for or that falls into our laps, as openly and as freely as possible, without giving in to the desire to copy for the sake of the security that every model, every guru seems to offer us?

It is the false security of models, step-by-step plans and copying from others that keeps organisations in their current place and position. By copying, organisations distinguish themselves less and less from each other in terms of structure, systems, competition and knowledge management. Organisations lack individuality and uniqueness. And that is a real pitfall.

Organisations that are open for different kinds of impulses, that step into the dynamics of inclusion, that keep observing freshly, enter into a flow of continuous progression. Everything sets everything in motion – in tune with the moment, free from previous ballast and including each and every inspiration in co-creation with everything and everyone involved – always resulting in new and transient shapes.

Of course, the models and visions of other people may be inspiring. Of course writers such as Jospeh Jaworski, Danah Zohar, Stephen Covey, Jim Collins, Peter Senge … are not by accident at the top of many a manager's list. Great thinkers provide inspiration, outlines and methods for organisational development. But never will the visions of one situation be fully applicable to another. Something entirely new will always surface, a new reality connected to the whole and matching the organisation's individuality.

THREE PRINCIPLES

Three principles may inspire you in making organisational development more playful, more authentic and more organic. Applying these principles will stimulate spontaneity in organisational development and prevent the progression which starts from the additive claim, is slowed down by periods of stagnation and is exclusive. Applying them will create development that is continuous, gives everything a chance and experiences fragments as parts of the whole.

The principles are: inspiration, co-creation and experimentation. Each principle is described here briefly, clearly, and lightly, inviting you to apply them as you feel appropriate.

Inspiration

Everything that exists inspires and contributes to motion: objective, subjective and fictitious things. Words, images, sounds, in short all of our senses provide input. Inspiration does not always have to be explicit. That which can be read between the lines, which accompanies us as a vague outline, which we don't know yet, which is invisible and intangible – everything may contribute.

The process of what you explicitly want and are able or not able to make, together with that which is implicit, always results in new shapes.

The following figure shows how inspiration can work and how it can lead to the development of authentic action and true wisdom in people, groups, organisations and even societies.

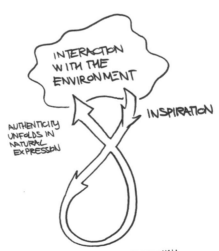

Co-creation

There are fundamental differences between creation and co-creation. Creation is making something new and presenting this result to the world as a given. Co-creation is about unconditionally offering whatever is in you to the process of creating with others. You give away all your ideas and thoughts and don't hold on to them, or defend them, so that they become part of the co-creation process.

Co-creation profoundly involves all of the players in a particular situation and opens up the possibility of generating motion which is bigger than the individual parts. What each part cannot establish on its own may be achieved through interplay. The players find themselves in a coherent flow towards the realisation of whatever may come to them.

Co-creation is different from negotiating, convincing, brainstorming, explaining, informing, finding support or arriving at a win win situation. It is the moment in which something entirely new is created through the interrelationship between people, or between people and other elements (for example, the environment, nature, books). One creates here and now, interlinked with the environment. And the very moment before, that creation had not existed. We talk about a unique new creation in a specific situation – be it a new meaning, a new form or even new matter.

Experimentation

Only experimentation can lead to fundamental innovation. Considering and experiencing each activity, each shape, every process as an experiment increases one's awareness of the continuous development in an organisation. Everything is in motion, not one single movement is the same as the previous. Everything takes shape in the moment and the given situation. Without experimentation, not one single idea would materialise. Every activity, every subject, decision or consideration has a unique meaning for the organisation.

These three principles are inseparably linked and continuously influence each other. Inspiration always incites creation, which incites experimentation, which accesses the world of inspiration and so forth. Sometimes fleetingly, sometimes robustly, sometimes fast, sometimes slowly, they follow each other, often hardly perceptible, but if you pay attention, always present. Sometimes these principles are applied in just a few seconds, sometimes they take weeks or months. The sequence in which the principles are applied varies too, and can be anything from coincidence to a conscious decision.

A UNIVERSE OF ENDLESS POSSIBILITIES

Like a scent from the past
Without really knowing
Gives you the security
Of how you experienced it
Or like every silence in your house
Tells you who is present and who isn't
I accept
Full of confidence a shard
A minute fragment
That touched me imperceptibly
Absolutely sure that the splinter
Will generously provide me evidence
Of its universality

LAB OF INSPIRATION
Godelieve Spaas

An open, playful and organic developmental process can be recognised by its unique constellation of apparent contradictions: the gentle disruption of boundaries, the tight navigation of a global course, the application of that which does not yet exist, organic structures.

The courage to encounter each other, to be connected with the environment, acting from values and a developing awareness of the variation in the meaning of things leads to beauty, organic growth, creative people, passionate contributions to the environment and a radiating presence in the world. In practise, this means a developmental approach that unfolds slowly but surely and in which people's growth goes hand in hand with the development of the company. An approach in which subtle, simple and nuanced activities or decisions often have a big impact.

Links with the outside world also affect development: an organisation is not alone in the world, but an important part of it. The external is internalised and vice versa. The customer participates in the brainstorming and unfolding, as does the provider, and sometimes even society: the government, interest groups, competitors and others.

EXAMPLES AS SOURCE OF INSPIRATION

We will present a few examples, real-life cases, that give a glimpse of how the three principles described above may be applied in the development of organisations and organisational structures, implicitly and explicitly.

We invite you to look beneath the outer appearance of these cases and open up to the deeper motion, the undercurrent flowing through these examples.

Some of the cases show very well how the original source of inspiration keeps surfacing, on its own or in combination with other sources, in the shape of the things that were created during the process.

The cases may inspire you to apply the principles in your own environment. You may want to create a change process in your own organisation, starting with new inspiration, real co-creation and original experiments.

LET'S MOVE!

SPORTSPECTRUM
The Importance of Remembering Your Ideals

After two years of careful preparation, the Dutch municipality of Alphen-aan-den-Rijn's sports department became an independent company: Sportspectrum. From that moment on the new company was responsible for profits and losses. It was now entirely up to the management, Kees van Veen and Peter Vrisekoop, to create an efficient organisation with the municipality as their main client.

Godelieve Spaas explains: 'I met them one year later. They weren't that happy with their new situation at all. Their main activities were encouraging people to work harder, better and faster on the one hand, and on the other to negotiate with their one and only client about prices over and over again. The instability of the local political situation and the ensuing risks were other issues to consider.

They had to decide on how to go further: evolving towards a lean and mean organisation, preparing for a take-over or creating a completely new concept to break out of this vicious circle.'

As Sportspectrum's core business is facilitating exercise, Kees and Peter went to the seaside for a couple of days to take some lengthy walks and do some brain exercise. Their hikes along the shore and the dunes brought them back to what they strongly believed in: inviting people to a lifetime of exercise and offering that possibility to everybody.

To achieve this goal they needed good sporting infrastructure (which they already had) and a lot of new initiatives and ideas to get people exercising. And most of all: money. They started to design their ideal organisation for the future.

They saw Sportspectrum as a hub between all parties involved with exercise and movement in society. They would build up knowledge and ideas and be like the spider in the web, connecting all parties and sharing knowledge about the vision of a healthy and flexible body, enjoying exercising, linking this to a healthy and open society. The involved parties include the municipality, companies, and all kinds of people and organisations with ideas and plans on physical exercise for groups of people.

Their motto: We are a reliable partner for everybody who wishes or has ideas to improve physical fitness. We want to be the best partner to co-create with and we offer a link between knowledge, exercising and social goals.

Enthusiasm

Peter and Kees initiated dialogues in their network to find out how to realise this. And by co-creating with their employees, their partners and new clients they found pathways towards solutions.

Instead of focusing on efficiency, they proposed a new deal to the local government: 'If we make a profit by working more efficiently, we will use that money to realise your goals. You want to increase the number of people that actively exercise. We will realise that by combining our knowledge, our fun in exercising and our social responsibility with your short and long term local policy.'

They made a similar proposal to the companies in the area: 'If you let us organise the sporting activities for your employees, we will make sure that our profit is used for creating more sporting activities in our community.'

Sportspectrum initiated all kinds of experiments to show their potential customers what to expect, like a swimming course to get fit for your skiing holiday, aqua dancing and a street football tournament.

For these experiments they asked their employees to join them in co-creating new concepts for exercising. They were invited to think and act along the same lines as the management: 'Go back to what you believe is good for you and good for society. Share your knowledge, your fun and your involvement, just like Sportspectrum does with its environment.'

The Situation Now

Sportspectrum is now an important partner for the municipality of Alphen-aan-den-Rijn. As an advisor, it evaluates the realisation and effectiveness of local policy on sports and exercise. Other local governments have shown their interest in becoming partners for facilitating and exploiting their sports facilities and activities. Several companies have asked Sportspectrum to organise sports activities for their employees. In this way they contribute to the vitality of their employees as well as to the local community.

The employees are growing in their new roles: taking initiatives, generating new concepts and working in co-creation with all kind of partners. And they are never afraid of sharing their knowledge with everyone who needs it, wants it or is interested. The habit of giving has become a main value in their company strategy.

ABOUT AFRICAN DANCE AND TRAVELLING IN THE HEART

HEEREMA MARINE CONTRACTORS
Leaving Comfort Zones when You Are Succesful

'I'm a senior marine engineer and what I've experienced the last 24 hours is hard to describe.

Yesterday evening I made music and danced to African rhythms with about 40 of my new colleagues, most of them male.

Before that we were talking about brain-dominant thinking styles and I came to understand that my thinking preference is rather rational and that I seek "control". I know now that I need to be offered more logical arguments in order to accept and go along with the new way of engineering we are opting for. I further understand that I want to see proof of those arguments in concrete plans, procedures and ways of working.

Last night I also talked to my colleagues about my car keys, which are very precious to me because they symbolise the fact that wherever I go I can enter my car and feel free to leave. I can deal with a lot of different situations but I always need to have something trustworthy with me in order to feel comfortable and secure. I never thought I was going to talk about my car keys and that they would tell so much about me. What is happening?

I am attending the "value starter" session of my Product Group. This morning I awoke at 6 am, after hardly four hours of sleep. We were asked not to speak to each other and to reflect on how we feel about the reorganisation: What are our worries and dreams? It is strange not to talk to each other and I wonder why this is so difficult? I never dream about my work. However I feel now that it is in my interest to get a better understanding of myself and how I respond to the changes. After a silent breakfast we all walked outside towards a pedestrian ferry that brought us to a small island. I heard a beating rhythm and after a short walk I saw a large tepee, smoke coming out of its open roof. I thought: "A tepee? What are we going to do?"

I entered the tepee with my whole team. We started working together a month ago after a reorganisation of our department. Now we were all sitting on a sheepskin around a fire in the middle of this tepee.

There was a kind of Indonesian priest who played a didgeridoo. For one hour we lay down to meditate to strange sounds and listened to a guided fantasy. At first I resisted and I saw that some of my colleagues felt very uncomfortable and others almost fell asleep.

Then I drifted away and wondered why we are doing this. Why are we invited to tell our worries and dreams? Why are we invited to help translate this vision about New Engineering into concrete solutions? Isn't this the task of management? Are they going to listen to my ideas? Will it be possible to implement the system I developed for myself within the whole department?

Then our Engineering Manager started to speak. It surprised me that he also expressed his doubts and is not sure about how to accomplish all the innovations within the organisation. He invited others to speak up and was not challenging their opinions. Then more people began to speak. I still hesitate and don't speak out yet, but I feel this is a dialogue I have never experienced before within our technology department.'

Heerema Marine Contractors (HMC) operates in the offshore oil and gas industry. HMC is one of the world's leading marine contractors in transporting, installing and removing all types of offshore facilities. HMC's services encompass overall management, including that of subcontractors, all logistics, planning, engineering and work preparation.

HMC is very successful and we know the old saying, 'Never change a winning team.' Despite their success they decided to fundamentally reconsider the way they worked and their organisational set-up.

Maarten Swinkels (new shoes today): 'We were invited by the Technology Department of HMC to help them in realising five fundamental organisational innovations. They have offices in Leiden (the Netherlands) and Houston (USA). With about 250 people they do the engineering for all transport, installation and removal projects and tenders.

Together with HMC we took up the challenge to implement the following changes:
1. Transition from an organisation set up for seven technical disciplines towards a department with five product groups who carry out dedicated work for specific markets
2. Introduction of value-based engineering
3. Introduction of core competence leadership
4. Standardisation of engineering processes
5. Off-shoring the engineering

Taking Responsibility

These innovations were defined at a very conceptual level but now they had to be translated into concrete organisational structures and habits. Traditionally there is a strong hierarchy within this company. Engineers are mainly challenged for complex technical matters and are not bothered with organisational issues beyond the scope of their project. We decided to act differently and ask all employees to take responsibility for introducing innovations in the organisation and finding workable solutions for improving their engineering processes.

The existing mindset required a paradoxical approach that made people want to develop their own answers. There was a need for an approach that broke old patterns and was opposite to existing management practise and expectations, i.e. management with strong leadership that provides all the organisational answers.

The HMC Technology Department had asked me to organise a large-scale event in which the vision for the five changes mentioned above would be shared with all 250 engineers. I questioned this idea and proposed to make the 'design for change' a shared issue with the newly appointed department management. I also suggested making use of the new structure of product groups and organising team meetings in these product groups to create the new way of engineering together. This breaks the 'old' pattern in which (only) a special assigned project team dealt with the change and came out with their solutions.

Value Starters

In our opinion there is strong hidden thinking potential within the group of engineers. That's why we want to offer them a structure that provides a basis for the process of co-creation. The discussions with the engineering managers led to the idea of developing value starter sessions within each product group. At the start of the project all teams try to capture the value issues relevant to the change in their product group. We organised five value starters in the Netherlands and one in Houston. The value starter programme made it possible to recognise and explore issues on two axes:

1. With the 'IT' axis we can handle all 'tangible and rational' issue linked to the new organisation and the new way of engineering
2. The 'WE' axis help us to tackle all 'interaction and non logical' issues connected with working together in new teams and defining new interaction patterns and breaking with old routines.

'To travel is to live
Some travel in their car,
Some travel in their mind
What about travelling in the heart?'
Martinez

These were the words inviting all engineers to their specific value starter, a 24-hour programme. We spent the first 16 hours on understanding the 'change' and developing more awareness of what it means for each individual. During the next 8 hours we worked on self-identified and relevant issues. We organised the value starters in such a way that the engineers had to consider everything from a fresh point of view. Getting the participants out of their comfort zone is a symbol for the changes in working habits and structures. Co-creation was the central issue, reinventing together and experimenting with the new ideas. After the 24-hour meeting concluded, draft plans were processed in small teams, resulting in a Product Group plan on how to realise the changes.

Co-creation at Work

Now all kinds of initiatives are taken up in various teams. A recruitment group developed 60 ideas for HRM on how to improve the recruitment process; an initiative for predefined technical knowledge communities was launched; engineering scopes are standardised and a Shared Interest Network has started (an open, self-supporting network consisting of groups of people who share a common interest around technical and non-technical issues).

By sharing the responsibility of this innovation programme with all the engineers, the management of the Technology Department is breaking with the old culture. The sustainability of this approach will have to overcome the doubts, resistance and questions as to what this implies for the heavy project workload. It may take 2 years before management is able to fully harvest all of the productivity benefits from giving people room and responsibility beyond participation in technical projects. Management also has to gain faith in this new approach and has to refrain from too easily taking the lead again and thus hindering initiatives from engineers.

FRACTALS AND FLAVOURS
WELLANTCOLLEGE WESTVLIET
Variety for Successful Education

Society is changing rapidly. Until recently the school system educated students to find their way in an industrial or service oriented, efficient and demanding society. Knowledge transfer and the development of skills were mainly focussed on preparing them to work in small and large organisations.

These days many young people have new challenges to tackle. On the one hand they are confronted with a complex society with many social and economic structures, rules and regulations. But as the world is changing rapidly they also have to learn how to create their own lives in a world of endless possibilities. Both requirements should be part of the new educational concepts and content.

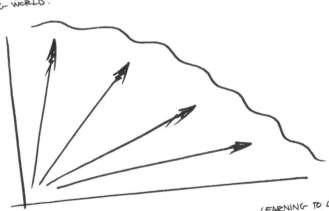

STARTING FROM INDIVIDUAL VISION & STRENGTH LEARNING TO PARTICIPATE & ADD VALUE IN A RECEIVING WORLD.

LEARNING TO LIVE IN & ADAPT TO A HIGHLY REGULATED (JUDGING) WORLD.

This story tells about teachers and managers of a technical and vocational school in The Hague who deeply recognise these new challenges and want to fundamentally change their educational methods. They strongly believe this is necessary in order to enable their students to really create a meaningful role for themselves in future society, fully based on their own talents and drives. Such a person will be able to find or create a genuine place, organisation or position that suits him/her best and where her/his added value is highest. It is a story of inspiration, co-creation and many, many experiments.

Dancing with Rogie & Co

Wellantcollege's general manager Peter Kranendonk and education manager Jos van Meegen initiated this project. They invited Rogie & Company, a dance group lead by Piet Rogie, to start up this innovation and change process. He is known in the world of dance for being a choreographer who organically creates new performances together with his dancers.

Piet and his dancers were invited to the school to show how they create a new choreography and how every dancer has her own role in it, all equally important, but very different at the same time. Teachers were invited to take part in this co-creation, to talk with the dancers, to deeply feel how this process works.

This experience inspired them to experiment with openness for variety as the main theme in their new educational concept. For six months, small groups of teachers and students started working and experimenting with different kind of learning methods and different combinations of content.

Finally they found out that they required a variety of methods to be able to teach all of the skills needed for the new world. They started experimenting on a broader scale. They had the students learn individually, in small groups and in big groups, inside the school and outside. Together with the students they decided what worked well and what didn't. Step by step they experimented, creating a wide variety of tools, lessons and so on.

Jos van Meegen explains: 'These experiments eventually led to an educational method that appeals to all different learning abilities, as is clarified in the following box. One can develop knowledge along different lines. On the one hand, we can look at the world as being objective, tangible, and discoverable through the senses. We can also look at the world as being subjective, designed from within, developed through one's own approach, from 'the meaning I give to my world.' On the other axis you will find the student as the consumer of this knowledge or as the producer of the learning process.'

This then gives four boxes with different content, styles, environments and tools of learning.

Teach: Traditional knowledge transfer, teacher to student
Search: Student explores and experiments to gain objective knowledge
Reflect: The teacher gives feedback on student's talents and skills
Quest: Student (co-)creates own knowledge and meaning

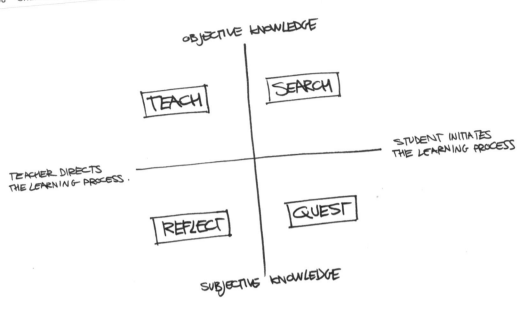

The Fractal Organisation

To make it possible for this educational concept to work on a larger scale, Wellantcollege had to achieve two other things. The teachers had to transform themselves, by developing totally new skills, by finding out what their hidden talents were and how to apply them, and by unlearning old and learning new teaching habits. Secondly, the school needed a new organisational structure that would fit this new educational method. Inspiration came through the study of fractals.

A fractal is a geometrical shape that is irregular at each scale of magnification. Hence it is always different in an infinite variation. At the same time, the whole consists of parts that repeat themselves at increasingly smaller scales.

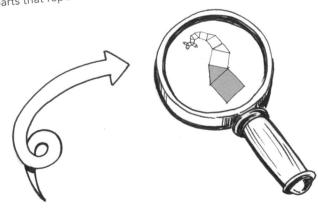

The particularity of fractals in geometry is that the shape of the parts is the same as that of the whole. The parts only distinguish themselves in size and colour. Hence, the shape of the whole can be recognised in each of the parts and vice versa. New and other similar shapes are created in the whole. In nature, fractals are an organising phenomenon through which order and chaos can go hand in hand.

The similarities between this school and fractals are the qualities of uniformity and maximum variety at the same time. Building a 'fractalized' institution could generate a fundamentally new dynamic, a new way of interacting with each other and shaping the services offered.

Peter Kranendonk and his management team decided to co-create everything around one basic form, with a fixed part and a varied part based on meaning. The organisation would then be shaped by interaction. Interaction around this basic form would 'define' the way in which things were developed and evaluated, the content of the tasks and roles, internal and external communication, the structure, the workplaces and the leadership style.

These figures display the basic shape: a fixed base and a meaning-based variation, which is in each part of the organisation and the dynamics of the whole.

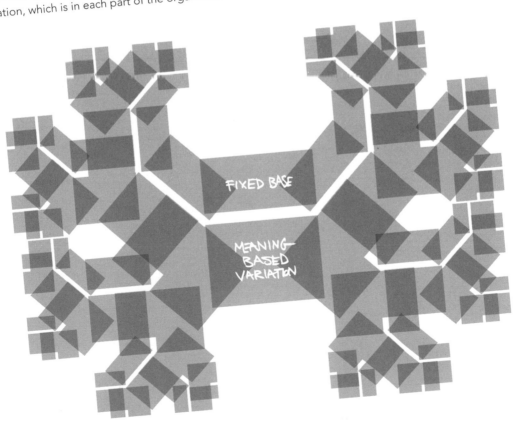

Freedom to Experiment, Freedom to Build

The Wellantcollege wanted each of its employees to act as freely as possible. They defined a number of interconnecting values, not to control each individual's activities but more as a kind of implicit frame of reference.

The institution's interconnecting values are:
- Variety in every organisational aspect is a vital condition for this educational concept
- Everyone fits in the whole in his/her own way
- We create a culture of giving and sharing
- Through dialogue we give meaning to our goals
- We grow in consciousness by elucidating the choices we make in our work

Peter and Jos decided to apply only a control-based management approach to the established minimum frameworks (the fixed base). For the rest, they trust in the autonomous self order that will arise from groups of employees with the most varied talents, interests and motivation.

Dialogues

To make the variable part – the subjective, often implicit part – effective, the variety of activities carried out by each individual has to be made explicit. This gives each activity meaning in the whole and creates cohesion. One can only achieve this by analysing each other's activities, putting them into words or images and holding onto them for a while. Hence, dialogues and interaction are needed so that people can state the intention behind their actions and explain why they chose to do things one way and not another. So there's a need for continuous dialogue about the deeper reasons for activities, the motives and their results.

These dialogues do not aim at the predictability of activities. They help to gain insight into the meaning of different activities, facilitating the creation of new forms, new talents, new variations.

The following figure gives a framework for dialogue about subjective (unique) actions.

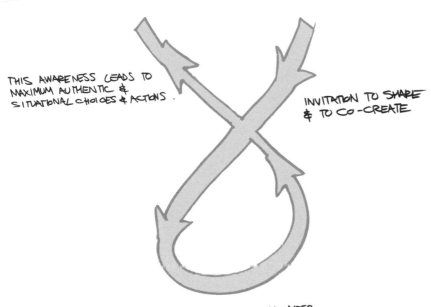

THIS AWARENESS LEADS TO
MAXIMUM AUTHENTIC &
SITUATIONAL CHOICES & ACTIONS.

INVITATION TO SHARE
& TO CO-CREATE

DIALOGUE LEADS TO AWARENESS
OF THE DRIVERS BEHIND
CHOICES & ACTIONS.

Everything concerning meaning is situational and hence flexible and change-able. Meaning is always created in co-creation. In co-creation a natural order unfolds that is in harmony with the whole. Trusting this process is crucial for the success of the dialogues.

Through dialogues about concrete choices, teachers and students are developing content and methods for a variety of means of knowledge transfer. This process doesn't take place overnight, but step by step, by talking, trying out, giving each other feedback and having the courage to make errors, looking at the same topics in new ways over and over again in order to discover new and different approaches, respond to them and try them out.

Situation Now

By putting these new organisational and educational models and methods into practise, the interactions between teachers, students, educational concepts are aligning more and more. Students indicate that they enjoy school much more than before.

And measurable results speak for themselves. Students in the new system score 1.5 points (out of 10) better than students in the traditional system, both on traditional knowledge tests and skills tests. And parents remark that their children have become more independent in taking initiatives outside school.

THE BEARABLE LIGHTNESS OF BEING

INAXIS

Creation in Dutch Government

InAxis is a programme for administrative innovation of the Dutch Ministry of Interior and Kingdom Relations. Nothing new here. Innovation is hot everywhere and you can find these programmes in governments all over the world. What is special is the radical approach InAxis has chosen.

Paul van Hal, director of the programme, describes the vision in ten principles:

- Practise is the source of inspiration
- The innovator retains ownership
- We don't have a focus, but we do focus
- We always make sure it keeps flowing
- Organise the energy towards yourself
- We do business with people, not with organisations
- We are not a knowledge centre
- The bearable lightness of being
- It's better to ask for forgiveness than permission
- Do, share and let go

Experiments

Paul van Hal: 'One of our cornerstones is facilitating and financing governmental organisational experiments, and letting them spread all over the Netherlands. An example of such an experiment is the small rural municipality of Ten Boer.

Many small municipalities use merging processes to upscale themselves. Ten Boer had a different idea. It decided to outsource operational tasks and a considerable portion of policy preparation tasks to the neighbouring, large city of Groningen. That left a core apparatus to organise policy preparation and outsourcing. Ten Boer thus keeps all its administrative responsibility and say over its set of tasks. The best of both worlds, a small scale for policy preparation and a large scale for operational tasks.'

Cherish the Nearling!

A feature of an experiment is that it does not always succeed, otherwise it would not be an experiment. But does that mean it's a failure? Not according to InAxis. Paul: 'There is something to be learned from every experiment, no matter what the results are. We've adopted the new word nearling* for this, a word for something that you have attempted but that did not lead to the desired result. The idea or plan is good but the circumstances have changed. Or a better option presents itself along the way. Or something goes wrong. Or there are suddenly different priorities.

The word nearling contributes towards enhancing a culture of innovation, of entrepreneurship, of the power of deeds. It places emphasis on the fact that initiatives are almost always worthwhile. Even if they do not lead to the desired result. You don't need to say that 'you made a mistake' or that 'it went awry'. No, you just say "you had a nearling".'

Reducing Risk Aversion

InAxis wants to improve conditions for innovation in public service. The programme for reducing risk aversion*, to achieve inhibition lowering is another sparkling example. 'In government, we often are overly averse to risk. To innovate, sometimes you have to go about your work less cautiously. Push the envelope of what is possible. Dare to do something that may go differently than you expect. Dare to do something that you may not have completely under control. That can sometimes fail. But you can learn so much from it, that new innovative ideas are the result.

Not only what you do is important, but also how you do it. These are two clarifications of our working principles:

We Work with People, not with Organisations

We have consciously chosen this approach, because when working with organisations you can lose a lot of time talking about positions and skills. We work with people who get things done and who are enthusiastic about turning ideas into reality. We think in terms of networks. Then the organisation will come along on its own accord when the time is right.

The Bearable Lightness of Being

Even if innovating is not always easy, it does not have to be as heavy as lead. We try when possible to opt for a light form and sometimes do not act normally. For example we had the nominees for the Dutch delegation of the 4th European Quality Conference introduce themselves to the judges' panel with a theatre show. They had the time of their lives and everyone was extremely enthusiastic.

Our attention also goes to reducing the administrative burden of government regulations. That may not sound like fun. But InAxis has started 'the Museum of Superfluous Policy'*, officially opened by the Minister of Interior in 2006, and exhibiting dozens of inspiring examples of unnecessary, contradictory, obsolete, complex, sometimes ridiculous rules and regulations – a playful and stimulating way to become aware of the need to abolish superfluous policy.'

* For more info on the nearling and reducing risk aversion, see the website www.nearling.com

EXCITING ONE MILLION CLIENTS

PGGM
Increasing the Creative Capacity of a Pension Fund

Martijn van Kooij is passionate about creativity and believes that any organisation uses only a small fraction of the creative potential of its employees. He works as Manager of Business Development and Innovation (BDI) for PGGM, the Pension Fund for Care and Welfare in the Netherlands. PGGM is a well known company with over one million customers and around 1100 employees. The company had defined five critical factors for success, one of them being the 'creative capacity' of the organisation. Martijn (BDI) and Ramon Vullings (new shoes today) laid out a programme: 'Increase the Creative Capacity of PGGM' based on 3 pillars.

- Developing attitudes and skills for creative thinking (culture)
- Getting inspiration and generating ideas (ideas)
- Putting ideas into action (implementation)

Attitude, Space, Initiatives

The usual way to organise large changes within PGGM is a top-down approach. For this programme, they decided to go bottom-up and let the employees explore and follow their own passion.

BDI did not want to focus on ideas, but on initiatives. People with ideas were encouraged to come into action. They were supported in developing their creative skills via a train-the-coach approach and were encouraged to change their working environment.

Key Activities in the Experiment were:

- 20 PGGM volunteers (who had attended a training programme for facilitating creative sessions) took up the task of 'change agent', helping the organisation with 'postponing judgement', increasing openness for new ideas
- Creative sessions aimed at process improvement and alternative products (pension solutions) were organised
- A new intranet site was developed as an inspirational environment, with quotes, images, cases of applied creativity from around the world, current initiatives within PGGM and a special innovation toolkit. Note that this was certainly not an idea management system. The intranet solution was aimed at sharing initiatives and linking people with passion in this large organisation
- Specific communications were set up: a creativity toolbox with quick reference cards, an irregular innovation newsletter and many physical inspirational items in the PGGM offices

Dream

A dream was put forward to trigger as many PGGM employees as possible. The dream was formulated as: 'Let's make the front page of the largest financial newspaper in the Netherlands with a PGGM innovation.'

But this is only one example. Many activities took place, from bringing together the top 100 people in the company for a World Café* meeting on values, to having poets 'rhyme' meeting minutes, having clowns into the work environment and having the top management brainstorm in an elderly home (the place where their 'real customers' reside). Opening up the attitude towards change was the goal.

The front page was a bit out of league, yet PGGM did manage to make the third page of Het Financiële Dagblad with one of their new initiatives, the development of a pension in kind – a pension not just based on money, but also partly on services – which is now one of PGGM's on-going developments.

Looking back at the process these were the major learning points:

- Start with a small team who believe they can change things
- Make sure you make initial successes and added value visible to the organisation
- Acknowledge 'nearlings' and continue to share them throughout the whole organisation
- Work bottom-up. Individual passion helps to overcome internal hurdles
- Make sure creativity is a means, not an end in itself
- Keep focusing on 'giving space' for new initiatives and allowing experiments, knowing you need some nearlings to generate success

*A World Café conversation is a creative process for leading collaborative dialogue, sharing knowledge and creating possibilities for action in groups of all sizes. See www.theworldcafe.com

PROUD TO BE DIFFERENT!

DRECHTWERK
Paradigms Shift in Social Economy

Drechtwerk is a company with and for special people. Founded in the 1970s as an organisation for people distanced from the labour market, mainly because of physical and/or mental disability, it grew into a company of 2000 people. They work in several departments with activities ranging from a metallurgical factory, catering, packaging... to the cultivation of plants.

The company became trapped in the dilemma of being commercial versus being social, a difficult stretch in the current timeframe where these two themes are more and more interconnected. And as in every business, the challenges and necessary changes are big. Production is under pressure. Prices are dropping. Government is reducing subsidies. The building, machinery and working habits have become outdated.

The figures had already gone into the red some years ago. All financial and organisational 'short term tricks' had been implemented. Enthusiasm for the future was very low. Only a fundamental turnaround could save the company.

Peter Kuipers, interim manager, explains: 'When I arrived at Drechtwerk it was clear to me that the challenge for this turn around was huge and that it couldn't be achieved in the "usual way": by cost-cutting, closing down some departments, reshuffling hundreds of people. And it's also obvious that laying off part of the workforce is not an option in this organisation. So we had to make this company profitable again and keep all the people on board.

The answers came to me from within the company. Our inspiration is the people themselves, their cheerfulness, their disarming honesty, their firm desire to prove their abilities, despite years of discouraging reorganisations.

I have never worked in a company where people are so special and inspiring. And they deserve better.'

New shoes today was invited to help facilitate a radical change in the organisational structure and policies. From now on we would build on the strengths and development skills of the individuals and groups, and link them with current market needs.

Two major paradigm shifts were introduced:
1. The only way to cope with these issues is to look at the problem on a bigger scale than company scale alone. We redefined the challenge from 'Let's create regular work for people with a handicap' into 'How can we let the world share in the added value of these people?'
2. As long as we regard the company as being part of civil service, they will never develop entrepreneurial drive. So we chose two values as underlying forces for the process of change
   - Dare to experiment
   - Dare to dream and become a hero

Kick-off

We started with a surprise meeting, gathering 40 people from all over the company and letting them experience the energy that an experiment is able to generate. The driving force would not be plans, everlasting meetings, perfectionism, budgets and overall visions, but acting today, experimenting, building on hidden potential and inviting as many people as possible to help realise the turnaround.

Everybody was presented a target just a little too high to reach in an easy way, but always within the scope of their talents. This represented the (short term) challenge. Countless new activities, products, services were tried out. New ways of monitoring the development of workforce skills. Splitting up the big company into 10 new companies. Tearing down some parts of the building and rebuilding new facilities. Negotiating new contracts with the local municipalities. Setting up joint development learning projects with a local engineering school.

Some innovations were successful, many weren't. But the overall result is new energy with all parties involved. And a turnaround in the figures, putting us back in the black.

New activities also mean new ways of communicating about the change:
- near the canteen we created the 'inspiration lane', a major corridor which was painted brilliant red and where all of the departments put up showcases of their latest innovations
- a musical brainstorming session with the workforce to get ideas on how to approach municipalities as clients
- the 'Nearling of the Month Award' to get accustomed to the attitude that it's better to make a mistake than to do nothing
- celebrating new successful activities with as many collaborators as possible inviting all neighbouring companies to a big nice-to-know-you-BBQ...

It took a few months to change the mood from cynical to hesitant to enthusiastic. But what's most important, we started to question some of the fundamentals the company was built on. A paradigm shift is on the way.

Your Dream

The next step was to invite people to bring in their own dreams as a basis for further action – the dreams of all employees, dreams of middle management, dreams of managers.

When we asked the workers what they would like to offer to the people in the city, some of them said: 'We would like to make them smile.' It is a nice example of the exact opposite of the mainstream attitude in our social economy. These people are not deplorable. They deserve to be brought back into society, into the economy, to be able to add their special value, to bring in that which makes them different.

Then we asked the managers, and they came up with a new vision for the future: several independent companies, cooperating with or joining other companies, who insure a healthy mix in the workforce, who monitor and promote the development of a higher degree of independence in the workforce, with all parties participating in developing and emancipating the mind and the activities.

Become a Hero

Managers were invited to become leaders of this process of change, to step into the light and make their dreams come true. To facilitate this transformation we used 'the path of the hero' inspired by Joseph Campbell.

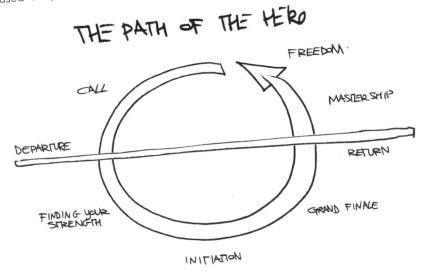

Thirteen managers are opening up to their 'hero potential' and are taking up leadership for a new company under the umbrella of the Drechtwerk Group. Here's how they have experienced their hero programme. Daphne Uyterlinde: 'I know now that when I change myself, I change the organisation.' Erwin Van Schaick: 'At first the programme acted as a mirror for my current role within Drechtwerk but now it brings me to a deeper level. It leads me to the question of what is my personal calling in this world…'

As Einstein said: 'Problems are not solved at the level of thinking that caused the problems in the first place.' To solve the problems of social economy we need thinking and acting on a deeper and broader level, we need a paradigm shift.

LEARN FROM YOUR NEARLINGS

NEW SHOES TODAY
Soul Mates Experimenting on the Edge of Creation, Innovation and Change

Thirteen people met professionally to initiate an organisation that matches with their own ideals and is in itself an example of what they want to show to the world. Paradigms are shifting.

From Scarcity to Abundance

The moment we understand that wisdom, power, love, knowledge, trust, authenticity… can only grow, we can share them endlessly without losing anything. These values do not converge with the zero sum principle. By sharing, we all gain more and more for everybody. Let's make a start by giving instead of taking what we can get, or measuring what we give against what we receive.

From Creation to Co-creation

The art of giving is also a starting point for co-creation. The most valuable creation is co-creation because two (or more) parties realise new added value for each other and the world at the same instant. And the only creation that exists is here and now, in an ever-changing world.

From Creating the Parts to Receiving the Wholeness

Everything is connected to the wholeness. Once you understand this you can fundamentally change your ways of intervening in the world and in organisations. When you experience the wholeness, you know that a tiny little change, a new perspective, a surprising activity may provoke crucial differences for the whole. It also means that borders between organisations, structures, cultures are not as closed as we may suspect. Everything is linked.

These paradigm shifts are progressing. As time goes by they will find their own new forms, including the existing ones. So scarcity will be part of the new paradigm of abundance.

BORDERS FADING.

CLOSED BORDERS → OPENING UP → MERGING IN A NEW WAY

Co-creating an Organisation

In the heart of that change these thirteen people initiated an organisation to contribute to those shifts: to find invigorating forms, radically new angles, fresh perspectives, new applications, authentic concepts, inspiring products, and most of all: new ways of doing business. And they want to act today. It's not about making plans. It's about acting here and now, with respect for history and with care for the future and for the whole.

They are co-creating an organisational form based on these shifting paradigms. Their main goals are to maximise the authenticity and personal growth of all the participants, to connect from soul to soul internally and with clients, to increase consciousness for a better world.

Instead of becoming a closed, well defined organisation they choose to be a diffuse and organic, very open organisation. Merging with others, without hierarchy, and giving space to everybody, to every idea and many, many activities.

DIFFUSE ORGANIZATIONAL FORMS

TRADITIONAL HIERARCHY

TO AN ACCUMULATION OF PERSONAL ADDED VALUES.

Nurturing the Soul

If an organisation is so diffuse and continuously changing you have to har-vest your activities, share your experiences, continuously examine processes and dilemmas. It is the only way to render the collective soul explicit, to make it tangible, to hold it for a while and treasure it. You need to evaluate your actions and connect with your ideas, your dreams, your growth.

In order to do so, the crew of new shoes today use the following circles to question themselves, their activities and their impact on the environment. By developing awareness on these three levels they nurture their own souls and the soul of new shoes today.

There are three main themes in the circles.

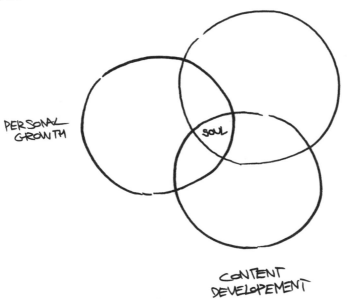

PERSONAL GROWTH

INTERACTION WITH & ADDING TO THE ENVIRONMENT.

SOUL

CONTENT DEVELOPEMENT

New Ways of Organising

Let's give some examples of how all this works in practise.

Everybody is able to start up whatever project in the field of creation, innova-tion and change. When working in the market place, co-creation is the first reflex for all activities, with a unique combination of the new shoes today crew, soul mates and clients. All today-activities are set up as a project and the goal is always to create something entirely new with and for all participants involved.

The new shoes today crew meet once a month during a 'WonderWalk', an original way of meeting while hiking through the countryside. Surprising how all the goals of traditional meetings can be achieved while physically, emotionally and spiritually enjoying nature or another environment.

Nobody owns the company or the label, since the founders have decided to pay no dividends and not to accumulate money in the organisation. Nobody is on the payroll. Everybody is an entrepreneur. The structure is as virtual and flexible as possible in order to reach the above-mentioned targets. When difficult organisational decisions have to be made, everybody has an equal vote.

Internal roles (ICT, accounting, content development, PR, publications…) are taken on by whoever thinks they are best at it, and are rewarded by an internal fee for the project. The role is up for discussion at any moment if someone thinks they can do better.

The previous cases were co-created and described by new shoes today crew and soul mates.
- Sportspectrum: Godelieve Spaas
- Heerema Marine Contractors: Maarten Swinkels and Gabriël Augustijn
- Wellantcollege Westvliet: Godelieve Spaas and Ellis Oudendijk
- InAxis: Igor Byttebier and Ramon Vullings
- PGGM: Ramon Vullings
- Drechtwerk: Igor Byttebier and Godelieve Spaas

A year from now, you may wish you had started... TODAY
Karen Lamb

INSPIRATION FOR THE ROAD

Ready for the adventure?

Three websites which will help you on your road to creativity:

creativitytoday.net

Sharing the road with others is much more fun than travelling alone. You can meet other readers of *Creativity Today* on the website. You will also be able to download creativity tools and get linked to the global creativity community, which will bring you into contact with other readers, thinkers and doers. On the website of *Creativity Today* you can submit comments and suggestions regarding this book. It provides more information about the authors and you can also order books there.

The book is A KEY; when you actually have a copy of this book, a secret login code can be found within it to gain access to additional materials and resources... Visit the website for the instructions.

nearling.com

When putting your creative skills into practise, you will go at it with passion. While trying, testing and developing you will encounter many nearlings. A nearling is a positive word for something new that you did with the right intentions, which has not (yet) let to the right result. Check page 165 for the full explanation of the nearling. Be inspired by others and share your own nearlings at the website.

newshoestoday.com

This is the digital hideout of new shoes today, the organisation co-founded by the writers of this book. New shoes today is a growing number of soul mates in business who give support to people and organisations on their road to creation, innovation and change. Together with clients, we take on 21st century challenges.

Our values are: open - drive - care - fun - unity - today.

We want to contribute in tomorrow's world and do this by counselling, coaching, product development, writing articles and books, organising meetings, co-creating things, supporting special people or ideas, or whatever comes to our minds.

Check the website for inspiration and support on your road to creation, innovation and change.

C I O D R N A T A A R C

C O D E A I T N A

R T O Y C D E A I T N A O R T O Y C E A

T N A O R D T O Y C A I T N A E O R D

O Y C I T N A E O A R D T O Y C I T N

E O A R O D T Y C T N A E O A I R O D

Y C N A E O A T I R O D T Y C A E O A

N I R O D T Y C A O A T N E I R O D T

C A O A N E I R T O D T Y C A A N E I R

O O D T Y C A N A E I R T O O D T Y C

N A E I R T T O O D Y C N A E I R T T O

O D Y C A E I R T N T O A O D Y C E A

R T N T O A O D Y C E A I O R T N T A

D Y C E A T I O R N T A O D Y C R E A T

O N T A O D Y C R E A T I O N T O D A

EXERCISES AND ANSWERS

Perception Exercise: Squares

Perhaps you found 17, 26 or 30 squares? For the time being, this is not important. What if we were to ask you to double the number you found? Does this seem impossible? Would you take the risk? We'll allow a few more minutes for this.

Tip. You will only succeed in this exercise if you are able to drop your thinking patterns. Try to realise which patterns guide your observation. Let go of them and search for a different kind of solution. For instance: How do you see and define 'square' now? Is there another way to see this?

How many squares do you see here?
When you are ready, read the comment on p. 233.

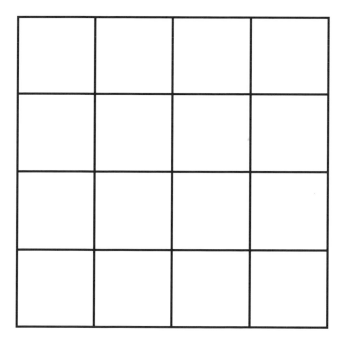

Caesar and Cleopatra – Presuppositions

What did you come up with? Suicide, or murder by poisoning? Shot through the window? Slipped and fell on the freshly washed wet floor? Actors in a heroic scene? You have undoubtedly thought of still other alternatives.

What happens in our brain when we are asked to solve this kind of question? We think associatively and we use our imagination. Inevitably we let words guide us in this process, words that are used in a certain context. These words help us further but they also force us into patterns. Sometimes it is useful to look for the 'presuppositions' on which the thinking patterns are built.

Ask yourself what patterns you are thinking in now. These are influenced by the key words in this story, like:

Crime author – glass – water – Caesar and Cleopatra

Try to put these words in another context. So? Have you come up with new ideas about the possible causes of death?

Go to page 234 and read the comment.

Queues at the Checkout – Reformulating

A good starting formulation helps to determine the success of a creative process. That is why it is important to know how to obtain the best formulation and to know what kind of problems are suitable for creative processes and which ones are not really suitable.

Several years ago, we dealt with this case at Albert Heijn supermarkets. The problem was broken down into two sub-problems. We organised two different creative sessions.

How can we reduce the waiting time at the checkout counters?
(The technical approach to the issue)
This session produced ideas such as: the customer scans the products himself; the invoice is sent to the customer's address; packing assistants posted at the checkouts; a scanner, similar to the security scanners you find in airports, scans all the products at once etc.

We have seen some of these ideas emerge at several distribution outlets.

How can we make waiting at the checkouts more pleasant?
(The psychological or marketing approach)
This session generated the following ideas: test products while you wait; carts with integrated walkmans; checkouts as information points with several themes (where people can watch a video for example); customers can talk or take a quiz about specific subjects; massages while waiting; etc.

As far as we know, this kind of idea has not yet been widely developed in practice.

We could have come up with different formulations. Have a look at the problem abstraction ladder on the next page. It shows you how to structure a problem. Asking 'What is the purpose?' brings you higher on the ladder. Asking 'In what ways?' brings you down a step on the ladder.

Problem Abstraction Ladder
HCW= How Can We?

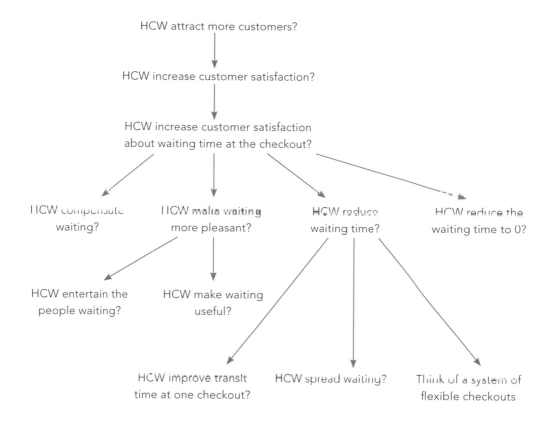

Peanuts
You put 2 peanuts in the first cup. Then you put the second cup on top of the first one and put three peanuts in it. In the first cup you have 2 + 3 = 5 peanuts. Put the 5 remaining peanuts in the third cup.

English and Scottish
The word is 'Scottish'.

Drawing of a Cow
This figure (drawn by Dallenbach) shows a close-up of a cow. Maybe you didn't recognise it at once. That made it easier to develop different visions. It is more important to notice that once you have indeed recognised the cow, it becomes more difficult to see something else. From now on 'the

cow' becomes dominant in your perception. The drawing has obtained significance. It is harder for your thoughts to become detached from it than before. That is how fast patterns grow. Return to the drawing now and experience the dominance of the cow.

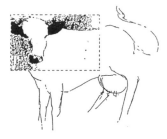

The Sum is 12
Thrice the same figure: 12 = 11 + 1

Sheriff John Timber
On Friday, the sheriff entered the village: Friday was the name of his horse.

Which of These Letters Does not Fit in?
A E I F U

Very often the answer is 'F', because it is the only consonant. Then of course we find ourselves in the grammar lesson. But when you postpone your judgement, you will see that all kinds of answers are possible:

A: has a closed space; is the only first letter of the alphabet; you have to open your mouth completely to pronounce it well; it has two legs on the ground; if you put it on its head it will topple ...
E: has three horizontal lines; E on its side becomes an M or a W; it is open on the right side; it can be the left half of the figure 8; ...
I: is the only one with a dot (lower case letters); is too early in the line if you look at alphabetical order; is the thinnest letter; is the only letter in the middle; is not found in the word UEFA ...
F: has the most irregular shape; is very unstable; the only one that makes us think of the 'F-word'; is too far in the line in terms of alphabetical order; you need to put a vowel in front to be able to pronounce it well; you can blow out a candle with it (got this one?) ...
U: is the only round shape; if it rains, it gets filled with water; is not found in the word facilitate; the only one found in the second half of the alphabet...

Equation
5 + 5 + 5 = 550
Solution: make a + into a 4
545 + 5 = 550 !

The Cod Fishers

Peter has gathered his family for a brainstorming session. This is what they have come up with. You certainly will have had some of these ideas yourself.

- another captain (hire someone if necessary)
- rent the boat
- sell that day's allowed share to a colleague
- look for another job, temporarily
- give the other captain advice through the radio on board
- fish for other kinds of fish, use different methods
- rent the boat to tourists
- enjoy a week of doing nothing

And it gets even crazier, they really have got the hang of it.

- put a buoy in the water, fix the net on one side and sail around the marker
- have a webcam installed and let Jan see what happens from his hospital bed; he can also pilot the ship
- fish with dynamite
- pull out the plug at sea

What did Peter finally do? Beware, this is a true story! He heard that another team was leaving the next day. He thought, 'What if I joined them so that we could fish with three boats and two nets instead of two boats and one net?' This had never been done before and it was quite a hard job convincing his colleagues. But eventually they tried. And the outcome? Fishing with three boats and two nets is far more efficient. If you have 2 boats and 1 net to catch 100 units, that's 50 per boat. You could (theoretically) catch 200 units with 2 nets in the same period of time. That's 66 units per boat. Furthermore, two boats are filled at once. In short, the fishermen valued this method so much that a large part of cod fishing is now done this way.

The moral we draw from this story is that you don't always have to wait for a problem to arise in order to find new solutions. Any cod fisher could have thought of this without John being ill. We are constantly surrounded by opportunities, but they only come into being at the moment we see them.

Animal Diagnosis (based on an article from Ode magazine)

If we don't consider whether you value this story or not (postponing judgement), you might draw the following opportunities from it:

- An institute for mentally disabled persons could start having a pet dog
- An interesting research topic for a student: Can this be proved?
- What kind of dog is best suited for these tasks?
- Would special training be useful, such as for police dogs or guide dogs?
- Who would organise it, and how?
- If I knew a socially challenged child, I would first take him or her to a dog training centre to see if contact with the animal would improve the situation and use this as a first step towards recovery.
- Perhaps a visit to a children's farm might also be a good idea for sick people?
- A series of TV-programmes or articles about special animals?

Some Suggestions for Vanessa

How can I find a nice companion for this trip?

How will I obtain interesting foreign contacts in the medical field?

How to convince my parents of the point of this trip?

How can I reduce my parents' concern?

How will I find a trainee post for myself abroad?

How can I find a sponsor for my trip?

How can I convince my mother, brother or sister to travel along with me for a while?

Weekend Trips

The first ideas for a nice weekend trip could be:

- a bicycle ride following a cycling route
- a walk along a river
- a visit to an amusement park with kids
- a swim in a subtropical swimming pool

Examples with Four Stimuli

Picasso

- a visit to a museum of contemporary art
- a visit to an artist's studio
- making a painting, guided by an artist
- a boat excursion on a river (via Picasso's Blue period)

Benedictine Monastery

- a visit to a monastery or a monastic order
- beer tasting evening or beer happening
- a walking tour along a pilgrim's route, with historical explanations
- a visit to a brewery

Watch
- a visit to a clockmaker
- a car rally or a search game in a city, with the challenge of precise timing
- a 24-hour happening, from Saturday 4 pm to Sunday 4 pm
- a visit 'back in time' to places in the collective memory of the group

Mars
- a visit to a meteorological institute (the planet Mars)
- develop a 'candy'-route (a Mars bar)
- make candy with the kids
- organise a paintball match (Mars is the god of war)

Presuppositions about a Second-hand Car Might Be:
- you are not the first driver
- the quality is not as good as that of a new car
- the mileage cannot be trusted
- this is about a car
- the car has already been driving
- the car is a few years old
- the car is still able to drive
- can the salesman be trusted?
- you buy a complete car (not parts of the car);
- you buy the car to drive it
- etc.

Socks from the Drawer
Maximum of 3: If the first sock is red and the second is blue (or the other way round), the third sock will be either red or blue and you will have a pair.

Ten Glasses in a Row
You take the second full glass, empty it into the second empty glass and put it back. You pour the fourth full glass into the fourth empty glass. Put it back and bingo: full-empty-full-empty-full-empty-full-empty-full-empty.

Perception Exercise: Squares
Were you able to double your number of solutions?
You can only succeed if you are willing to look for the thinking patterns that are guiding you now and let them go temporarily. We will give some solutions. You may have come up with others.

How many squares do you see here?
- Of course you can see the big square and the 16 small ones.
- You can also see the squares made of 4 squares. There are 9 of them, if you don't forget the one in the middle.

- You can also see the squares made of 9 squares. There are 4 of these.
- But can you also see the little black squares (between 4 white angles) on every crossing? There are 9 in the middle and if you want, another 16 on the borders.
- Can you find some depth in this square? Then every square hides more squares behind it, endlessly perhaps.
- And if you don't look at the picture, but at the text above it, you will find the word 'square', even 'squares', which add to the others.

Possibly you have come up with some more!
Maybe your reaction will be 'but that was not the question', or 'if this is allowed, then I can imagine more of these!' That's exactly the point. Are you able to recognise your own thinking patterns and let go of them to find new points of view?

You can develop this attitude (see p. 26, Postponing Judgement). The use of creative thinking techniques will help you conceive more new ideas faster and also to generate different kinds of ideas. You will always be able to double the number of ideas when you apply these techniques.

Caesar and Cleopatra

There is a good chance that we will think of Caesar and Cleopatra as historical figures, and certainly as people.

In this particular case, Caesar and Cleopatra were goldfish belonging to the author's aunt. She hadn't closed the window properly before going out shopping. The wind blew it open, causing the aquarium with the two gold-fish to fall to the ground. Caesar and Cleopatra didn't survive; they died after only a few minutes.

Other solutions are also possible. There is no such thing as one correct answer. It is, however, interesting to ask yourself what thinking patterns are framing your thoughts. The 'Presuppositions' technique on p. 85 will teach you how to become conscious of these patterns and how you can step out of them more easily.

Marc Heleven

Dennis Luijer

Gabriël

Willem Stortelder

Cyriel Kortleven

Rudolf van Wezel

Jan Bommerez

Vanessa Paterson

Justin Douglas

Karen Van Heuckelom

Marc Raison

Kathleen Steegmans

Nicole van den Bosch

THANK YOU

Zusje Helderman

Jane Bemont

Joost Kadijk

Maarten Swinkels

Casper Helder

Linda Corstjens

Oegnar Wedendorff

Julie Arts

Hans Veldink

Loesje

Michele Hutchison

Jim van de Beuken

Devon Reid

You

Gert Dijs

LITERATURE LIST

Creativity Today

Arden, Paul. *It's Not How Good You Are, It's How Good You Want to Be.* Phaidon Press, 2003

Chesbrough, Henry. *Open Innovation.* Harvard Business School Publishing Corporation, Harvard, 2003

Csikszentmihalyi, Mihaly. *Creativity: Flow and the Psychology of Discovery and Invention.* HarperCollins Publishers, New York, 1996

De Bono, Edward. *Lateral Thinking.* Pelican Books, London, 1970

De Bono, Edward. *Opportunities.* Penguin Books, London, 1980

Fletcher, Alan. *The Art of Looking Sideways.* Phaidon Press, London, 2001

Florida, Richard. *The Rise of the Creative Class.* Basic Books, New York, 2002

Gladwell, Malcom. *The Tipping Point.* Little, Brown and Company, London, 2000

Greenfield, Susan. *Brainstory.* Bosch en Keuning, Baarn, 2001

Handy, Charles. *The Empty Raincoat.* Hutchinson, London, 1994

Harvard Business Essentials: *Managing Creativity and Innovation.* Harvard Business School Publishing Corporation, Harvard, 2003

MacLennan, Nigel. *Opportunity Scouting.* Gower, Alderschot, 1994

Markham, S.K.. *'A Longitudinal Examination of How Champions Influence Others to Support Their Projects'* in: Journal of Product Innovation Management. Vol. 15, 1998

Mc Kim, Robert H. *Thinking Visually, a strategy manual for problem solving.* Wadsworth Belmont, USA, 1980

Peters, Tom. *Re-magine!* Dorling Kindersley Limited, London, 2003

Samuels, Mike, et al. *Seeing with the Mind's Eye, the history, techniques and uses of visualisation.* Random House, New York, 1997

Tanner, David. *Total Creativity in Business and Industry.* Advanced Practical Thinking Inc, New York, 1997

Creation Today

Barrett, Richard. *Building a Values-Driven Organisation.* Butterworth-Heinemann, 2006

Barrett, Richard. *Liberating the Corporate Soul.* Butterworth-Heinemann, 1998

Collins, Jim. *Good to Great.* Harper Business, 2001

Covey, Stephen R. *The 8th Habit.* Free Press, 2005

Goleman, Daniel. *Emotional Intelligence.* Bloomsbury, 1996

Goleman, Daniel, Annie McKee & Richard Boyatzis. *The New Leaders.* Little, Brown Book Group, 2003

Jaworski, Joseph. *Synchronicity.* Berrett-Koehler Publishers, 1996

Krishnamurti, J. & David Bohm. *The Limits of Thought / Discussions.* Routeledge, 1999

Senge, Peter M., et al. *The Fifth Discipline Fieldbook.* Nicholas Brealey Publishing, 1994

Senge, Peter, Joseph Jaworski & Otto C. Scharmer. *Presence.* Nicholas Brealey Publishing, 2005

Wheatley, Margaret J. *Leadership and the New Science.* Berrett-Koehler Publishers, 2001

Wilbur, Ken. *A Theory of Everything.* Shambhala Publications, 2001

Zohar, Danah & Ian Marshall. *Spiritual Intelligence.* Bloomsbury Publishing PLC, 2001

Zohar, Danah. *Spiritual Capital.* Bloomsbury, 2005

INDEX